ARTIFICIAL INTELLIGENCE

Notes

Rahul Basu

By Rahul Basu

Foreword

These notes were put together to make Artificial Intelligence approachable to students meeting the subject for the first time within the VTU curriculum. Rather than paraphrasing a textbook, the aim throughout has been to explain each idea in plain language, work through the classic examples carefully, and connect the theory to code wherever it helps the ideas stick.

The material follows the sequence prescribed by the VTU syllabus, moving from foundational search and knowledge-representation problems through to learning algorithms, neural networks, and probabilistic reasoning. Wherever a topic tends to cause confusion during exam preparation, an additional worked example or a short piece of Python has been included alongside the theory.

The exercise-solving section towards the end mirrors previous VTU question papers, organised module by module, so that concepts can be revised in the same order in which they are typically examined.

I hope these notes serve you well, whether you are working through the syllabus for the first time or revising before an examination.

Rahul Basu

Introduction

Artificial Intelligence is concerned with building systems that behave, to some useful degree, intelligently: systems that can search through possibilities, represent and reason about what they know, learn from experience, and act under uncertainty. This set of notes is organised to build up these ideas in a natural order.

The first three chapters set the groundwork: what intelligence and AI techniques actually mean, how problems can be framed as search through a problem space, and how heuristics make that search practical. Chapter 4 turns to knowledge representation – the question of how facts, rules, and relationships can be captured in a form a program can reason over.

Chapters 5 through 9 cover machine learning in the order it is usually taught: concept learning and the FIND-S / Candidate-Elimination algorithms, decision trees and ID3, neural networks and back-propagation, Bayesian learning, and finally the evaluation of learned hypotheses alongside instance-based learning and reinforcement learning.

Chapter 10 collects solved and partially solved exam-style questions, organised by the same five modules used in VTU examinations, for focused revision. Chapter 11 gathers the Python implementations referenced throughout the earlier chapters into one place, and Chapter 12 is an index for quick lookup.

Each chapter is largely self-contained, but reading them in order gives the clearest picture of how the ideas connect. Worked examples are included wherever a derivation or algorithm is easy to state but easy to get wrong in practice.

Artificial Intelligence Notes

Table of Contents

Concept Learning rewritten with ASCII-safe notation. Index added at end.

4. The following are the figures showing some of the tasks that are the targets of work in AI:

Mundane Tasks

- Perception
  - Vision
  - Speech
- Natural language
  - Understanding
  - Generation
  - Translation
- Commonsense reasoning
- Robot control

Formal Tasks

Games
- Chess
- Backgammon
- Checkers -Go

Mathematics
- Geometry
- Logic
- Integral calculus
- Proving properties of programs

Expert Tasks

- Engineering
  - Design
  - Fault finding
  - Manufacturing planning
- Scientific analysis
- Medical diagnosis
- Financial analysis

Perception of the world around us is crucial to our survival. Animals with much less intelligence than people are capable of more sophisticated visual perception. Perception tasks are difficult because they involve analog signals. A person who knows how to perform tasks from several of the categories shown in figure learns the necessary skills in standard order.

First perceptual, linguistic and commonsense skills are learned. Later expert skills such as engineering, medicine or finance are acquired.

Physical Symbol System Hypothesis

At the heart of research in artificial intelligence, the underlying assumptions about intelligence lie in what Newell and Simon (1976) call the physical symbol system hypothesis. They define a physical symbol system as follows:

1. Symbols
2. Expressions
3. Symbol Structure
4. System

A physical symbol system consists of a set of entities called **symbols**, which are physically patters that can occur as components of another type of entity called an **expression** (or symbol structure). A **symbol structure** is composed of a number of instances (or tokens) of symbols related in some physical way. At any instance of the time the **system** will contain a collection of these symbol structures. The system also contains a collection of **processes** that operate on expressions to produce other expressions: processes of creation, modification, reproduction and destruction.

They state hypothesis as:

> ***"A physical symbol system has the necessary and sufficient means for general 'intelligent actions'."***

This hypothesis is only a hypothesis there appears to be no way to prove or disprove it on logical ground so, it must be subjected to empirical validation we find that it is false. We may find the bulk of the evidence says that it is true but only way to determine its truth is by experimentation"

Computers provide the perfect medium for this experimentation since they can be programmed to simulate physical symbol system we like. The importance of the physical symbol system hypothesis is twofold. It is a significant theory of the nature of human intelligence and so is of great interest to psychologists.

What is an AI Technique?

Artificial Intelligence problems span a very broad spectrum. They appear to have very little in common except that they are hard. There are techniques that are appropriate for the solution of a variety of these problems. The results of AI research tells that

Intelligence requires Knowledge. Knowledge possesses some less desirable properties including:

- *It is voluminous*

- *It is hard to characterize accurately*
- *It is constantly changing*
- *It differs from data by being organized in a way that corresponds to the ways it will be used.*

AI technique is a method that exploits knowledge that should be represented in such a way that:

The knowledge captures generalizations. In other words, it is not necessary to represent each individual situation. Instead situations that share important properties are grouped together.

It can be understood by people who must provide it. Most of the knowledge a program has must ultimately be provided by people in terms they understand.

It can be easily be modified to correct errors and to reflect changes in the world and in our world view.

It can be used in a great many situations even if it is not totally accurate or complete.

It can be used to help overcome its own sheer bulk by helping to narrow the range of possibilities that must usually be considered.

It is possible to solve AI problems without using AI techniques. It is possible to apply AI techniques to solutions of non-AI problems.

Important AI Techniques:

- **Search:** Provides a way of solving problems for which no more direct approach is available as well as a framework into which any direct techniques that are available can be embedded.
- **Use of Knowledge:** Provides a way of solving complex problems by exploiting the structures of the objects that are involved.
- **Abstraction:** Provides a way of separating important features and variations from the many unimportant ones that would otherwise overwhelm any process.

Criteria for Success (Turing Test)

In 1950, **Alan Turing** proposed the method for determining whether a machine can think. His method has since become known as the **"Turing Test"**. To conduct this test, we need two people and the machine to be evaluated. Turing Test provides a definition of intelligence in a machine and compares the intelligent behavior of human being with that of a computer.

One person A plays the role of the interrogator, who is in a separate room from the computer and the other person. The interrogator can ask set of questions to both the computer Z and person X by typing questions and receiving typed responses. The interrogator knows them only as Z and X and aims to determine who the person is and who the machine is.

The goal of machine is to fool the interrogator into believing that it is the person. If the machine succeeds we conclude that the machine can think. The machine is allowed to do whatever it can do to fool the interrogator.

> *For example, if asked the question "How much is 12,324 times 73,981?" The machine could wait several minutes and then respond with wrong answer.*

The interrogator receives two sets of responses, but does not know which set comes from human and which from computer. After careful examination of responses, if interrogator cannot definitely tell which set has come from the computer and which from human, then *the computer has passed the Turing Test.* The more serious issue is the **amount of knowledge** that a machinewould need to pass the Turing test.

Overview of Artificial Intelligence

It was the ability of electronic machines to store large amounts of information and process it at very high speeds that gave researchers the vision of building systems which could emulate (imitate) some human abilities.

We will see the introduction of the systems which equal or exceed human abilities and see them because an important part of most business and government operations as well as our daily activities.

Definition of AI: Artificial Intelligence is a branch of computer science concerned with the study and creation of computer systems that exhibit some form of intelligence such as systems that learn new concepts and tasks, systems that can understand a natural language or perceive and comprehend a visual scene, or systems that perform other types of feats that require human types of intelligence.

To understand AI, we should understand

- ❑ Intelligence
- ❑ Knowledge
- ❑ Reasoning
- ❑ Thought
- ❑ Cognition: gaining knowledge by thought or perception learning

The definitions of AI vary along two main dimensions: thought process and reasoning and behavior.

AI is not the study and creation of conventional computer systems. The study of the mind, the body, and the languages as customarily found in the fields of psychology, physiology, cognitive science, or linguistics.

In AI, the goal is to develop working computer systems that are truly capable of performing tasks that require high levels of intelligence.

2. Problems, Problem Spaces and Search

Problem:

A problem, which can be caused for different reasons, and, if solvable, can usually be solved in a number of different ways, is defined in a number of different ways.

To **build a system or to solve a particular problem** we need to do four things.

1. Define the problem precisely. This definition must include precise specification of what the initial situation will be as well as what final situations constitute acceptable solutions to the problem
2. Analyze the problem
3. Isolate and represent the task knowledge that is necessary to solve the problem
4. Choose the best solving technique and apply it to the particular problem.

Defining the Problem as a State Space Search

Problem solving = Searching for a goal state

It is a structured method for solving an unstructured problem. This approach consists of number of states. The starting of the problem is "Initial State" of the problem. The last point in the problem is called a "Goal State" or "Final State" of the problem.

State space is a set of legal positions, starting at the initial state, using the set of rules to move from one state to another and attempting to end up in a goal state.

Methodology of State Space Approach

1. To represent a problem in structured form using different states
2. Identify the initial state
3. Identify the goal state
4. Determine the operator for the changing state
5. Represent the knowledge present in the problem in a convenient form
6. Start from the initial state and search a path to goal state

To build a program that could "**Play Chess**"

- we have to first specify the starting position of the chess board
    - Each position can be described by an 8-by-8 array.
    - Initial position is the game opening position.
- rules that define the legal moves
    - Legal moves can be described by a set of rules:
        - Left sides are matched against the current state.
        - Right sides describe the new resulting state.
- board positions that represent a win for one side or the other
    - Goal position is any position in which the opponent does not have a legal move and his or her king is under attack.

- We must make explicit the preciously implicit goal of not only playing a legal game of chess but also winning the game, if possible.

Production System

The entire procedure for getting a solution for AI problem can be viewed as "**Production System**". It provides the desired goal. It is a basic building block which describes the AI problemand also describes the method of searching the goal. Its main components are:

- A **Set of Rules**, each consisting of a left side (a pattern) that determines the applicability of the rule and right side that describes the operation to be performed if the rule is applied.
- **Knowledge Base** – It contains whatever information is appropriate for a particular task. Some parts of the database may be permanent, while the parts of it may pertain only to the solution of the current problem.
- **Control Strategy** – It specifies the order in which the rules will be compared to the database and the way of resolving the conflicts that arise when several rules match at one.
    - The first requirement of a goal control strategy is that it is cause motion; a control strategy that does not cause motion will never lead to a solution.
    - The second requirement of a good control strategy is that it should be systematic.
- **A rule applier:** Production rule is like below

```
if(condition) then
        consequence or action
```

Algorithm for Production System:

1. Represent the initial state of the problem
2. If the present state is the goal state then go to step 5 else go to step 3
3. Choose one of the rules that satisfy the present state, apply it and change the state to new state.
4. Go to Step 2
5. Print "Goal is reached " and indicate the search path from initial state to goal state
6. Stop

Classification of Production System:

Based on the direction they can be

1. Forward Production System
    - Moving from Initial State to Goal State
    - When there are number of goal states and only one initial state, it is advantage to use forward production system.
2. Backward Production System
    - Moving from Goal State to Initial State
    - If there is only one goal state and many initial states, it is advantage to use backward production system.

Production System Characteristics

Production system is a good way to describe the operations that can be performed in a search for solution of the problem.

Two questions we might reasonably ask at this point are:

- *Can production systems, like problems, be described by a set of characteristics that shed some light on how they can easily be implemented?*
- *If so, what relationships are there between problem types and the types of production systems best suited to solving the problems?*

The answer for the first question can be considered with the following ***definitions of classes of production systems***:

A **monotonic production system** is a production system in which the applications of a rule never prevents the later application of another rule that could also have been applied at the time the first rule was selected.

A **non-monotonic production system** is one which this is not true.

A **partially commutative production system** is a production system with the property that if the application of a particular sequence of rules transforms state X into state Y, then any permutation of those rules that is allowable also transforms state X into state Y.

A **commutative production system** is a production system that is both monotonic and partially commutative.

In a formal sense, there is no relationship between kinds of problems and kinds of production of systems, since all problems can be solved by all kinds of systems. But in practical sense, there definitely is such a relationship between kinds of problems and the kinds of systems that led themselves naturally to describing those problems.

The following figure shows the four categories of production systems produced by the two dichotomies, monotonic versus non-monotonic and partially commutative versus non-partially commutative along with some problems that can be naturally be solved by each type of system.

	Monotonic	**Non-monotonic**
Partially commutative	Theorem proving	Robot Navigation
Not Partially commutative	Chemical Synthesis	Bridge

The four categories of Production Systems

- Partially commutative, monotonic production systems are useful for solving ignorable problems that involves creating new things rather than changing old ones generally ignorable. Theorem proving is one example of such a creative process partially commutative, monotonic production system are important for a implementation stand point because they can be implemented without the ability to backtrack to previous states when it is discovered that an incorrect path has been followed.

- Non-monotonic, partially commutative production systems are useful for problems in which changes occur but can be reversed and in which order of operations is not critical.

This is usually the case in physical manipulation problems such as "Robot navigation on a flat plane". The 8-puzzle and blocks world problem can be considered partially commutative production systems are significant from an implementation point of view because they tend to read too much duplication of individual states during the search process.

- ❑ Production systems that are not partially commutative are useful for many problems in which changes occur. For example "Chemical Synthesis"
- ❑ Non-partially commutative production system less likely to produce the same node many times in the search process.

Problem Characteristics

In order to choose the most appropriate method (or a combination of methods) for a particular problem, it is necessary to analyze the problem along several key dimensions:

- Is the problem decomposable?
- Can solution steps be ignored or undone?
- Is the universe predictable?
- Is a good solution absolute or relative?
- Is the solution a state or a path?
- What is the role of knowledge?
- Does the task require human-interaction?
- Problem Classification

Is the problem decomposable?

Decomposable problem can be solved easily. Suppose we want to solve the problem of computing the expression.

We can solve this problem by breaking it down into these smaller problems, each of which we can then solve by using a small collection of specific rules the following figure shows problem tree that as it can be exploited by a simple recursive integration program that works as follows.

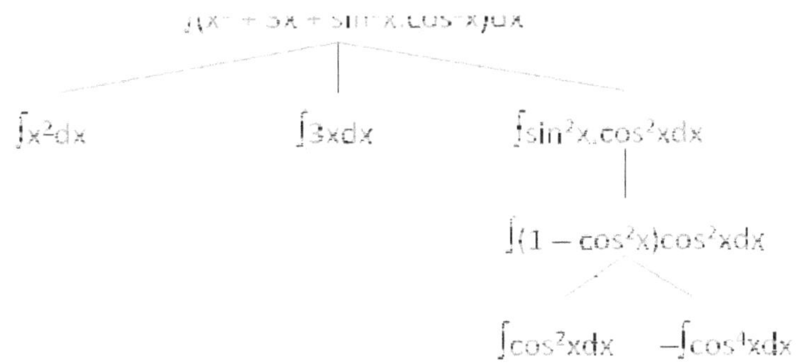

At each step it checks to see whether the problem it is working on is immediately solvable. If so, then the answer is returned directly. If the problem is not easily solvable, the integrator checks to see whether it can decompose the problem into smaller problems. It can create those problems and calls itself recursively on using this technique of problem decomposition we can often solve very large problem easily.

Can solution steps be ignored or undone?

Suppose we are trying to prove a mathematical theorem. We proceed by first proving a lemma that we think will be useful. A lemma that has been proved can be ignored for next steps as eventually we realize the lemma is no help at all.

Now consider the 8-puzzle game. A sample game using the 8-puzzle is shown below:

In attempting to solve the 8 puzzle, we might make a stupid move for example; we slide the tile 5 into an empty space. We actually want to slide the tile 6 into empty space but we can back track and undo the first move, sliding tile 5 back to where it was then we can know tile 6 so mistake and still recovered from but not quit as easy as in the theorem moving problem. An additional step must be performed to undo each incorrect step.

Now consider the problem of playing chess. Suppose a chess playing problem makes a stupid move and realize a couple of moves later. But here solutions steps cannot be undone.

The above three problems illustrate difference between three important classes of problems:

1) **Ignorable:** in which solution steps can be ignored.
   Example: Theorem Proving
2) **Recoverable:** in which solution steps can be undone.
   Example: 8-Puzzle
3) **Irrecoverable:** in which solution steps cannot be undone.
   Example: Chess

The recoverability of a problem plays an important role in determining the complexity of the control structure necessary for problem solution.

Ignorable problems can be solved using a simple control structure that never backtracks. ***Recoverable problems*** can be solved by slightly complicated control strategy that does sometimes make mistakes using backtracking. ***Irrecoverable problems*** can be solved by recoverable style methods via planning that expands a great deal of effort making each decision since the decision is final.

Is the universe predictable?

There are certain outcomes every time we make a move we will know what exactly happen. This means it is possible to plan entire sequence of moves and be confident that we know what the resulting state will be. Example is 8-Puzzle.

In the uncertain problems, this planning process may not be possible. Example: Bridge Game – Playing Bridge. We cannot know exactly where all the cards are or what the other players will do on their turns.

We can do fairly well since we have available accurate estimates of a probabilities of each of the possible outcomes. A few examples of such problems are

- Controlling a robot arm: The outcome is uncertain for a variety of reasons. Someone might move something into the path of the arm. The gears of the arm might stick.
- Helping a lawyer decide how to defend his client against a murder charge. Here we probably cannot even list all the possible outcomes, which leads outcome to be uncertain.

- *For certain-outcome problems, planning can used to generate a sequence of operators that is guaranteed to lead to a solution.*
- *For uncertain-outcome problems, a sequence of generated operators can only have a good probability of leading to a solution.*
- *Plan revision is made as the plan is carried out and the necessary feedback is provided.*

Is a Good Solution Absolute or Relative?

Consider the problem of answering questions based on a database of simple facts, such as the following:

1) Marcus was a man.
2) Marcus was a Pompeian.
3) Marcus was born in 40 A.D.
4) All men are mortal.
5) All Pompeian's died when the volcano erupted in 79 A.D.
6) No mortal lives longer than 150 years.
7) It is now 1991 A.D.

Suppose we ask a question "Is Marcus alive?" By representing each of these facts in a formal language such as predicate logic, and then using formal inference methods we can fairly easily derive an answer to the question.

Since we are interested in the answer to the question, it does not matter which path we follow. If we do follow one path successfully to the answer, there is no reason to go back and see if some other path might also lead to a solution. These types of problems are called as "Any path Problems".

Now consider the Travelling Salesman Problem. Our goal is to find the shortest path route that visits each city exactly once.

Suppose we find a path it may not be a solution to the problem. We also try all other paths. The shortest path (best path) is called as a solution to the problem. These types of problems are known as "Best path" problems. But path problems are computationally harder than any path problems.

Is the solution a state or a path?

Consider the problem of finding a consistent interpretation for the sentence

The bank president ate a dish of pasta salad with the fork

There are several components of this sentence, each of which may have more than one interpretation. Some of the sources of ambiguity in this sentence are the following:

- The word "Bank" may refer either to a financed institution or to a side of river. But only one of these may have a President.
- The word "dish" is the object of the word "eat". It is possible that a dish was eaten.
- But it is more likely that the pasta salad in the dish was eaten.

Because of the interaction among the interpretations of the constituents of the sentence some search may be required to find a complete interpreter for the sentence. But to solve the problem of finding the interpretation we need to produce only the interpretation itself. No record of the processing by which the interpretation was found is necessary. But with the "water-jug" problem it is not sufficient to report the final state we have to show the "path" also.

So the solution of natural language understanding problem is a state of the world. And the solution of "Water jug" problem is a path to a state.

What is the role of knowledge?

Consider the problem of playing chess. The knowledge required for this problem is the rules for determining legal move and some simple control mechanism that implements an appropriate search procedure.
Now consider the problem of scanning daily newspapers to decide which are supporting 'n' party and which are supporting 'y' party. For this problems are required lot of knowledge.

The above two problems illustrate the difference between the problems for which a lot of knowledge is important only to constrain the search for a solution and those for which a lot of knowledge is required even to be able to recognize a solution.

Does a task require interaction with the person?

Suppose that we are trying to prove some new very difficult theorem. We might demand a prove that follows traditional patterns so that mathematician each read the prove and check to make sure it is correct. Alternatively, finding a proof of the theorem might be sufficiently difficult that the program does not know where to start. At the moment people are still better at doing the highest level strategies required for a proof. So that the computer might like to be able to ask for advice.
For Example:

- Solitary problem, in which there is no intermediate communication and no demand for an explanation of the reasoning process.
- Conversational problem, in which intermediate communication is to provide either additional assistance to the computer or additional information to the user.

Problem Classification

When actual problems are examined from the point of view all of these questions it becomes apparent that there are several broad classes into which the problem fall. The classes can be each associated with a generic control strategy that is approached for solving the problem. There is a variety of problem-solving methods, but there is no one single way of solving all problems. Not all new problems should be considered as totally new. Solutions of similar problems can be exploited.

PROBLEMS

Water-Jug Problem

Problem is "You are given two jugs, a 4-litre one and a 3-litre one. One neither has any measuring markers on it. There is a pump that can be used to fill the jugs with water. How can you get exactly 2 litres of water into 4-litre jug?"

Solution:

The state space for the problem can be described as a set of states, where each state represents the number of gallons in each state. The game start with the initial state described as a set of ordered pairs of integers:

- State: (x, y)
  - x = number of lts in 4 lts jug
  - y = number of lts in 3 lts jug

    x = 0, 1, 2, 3, or 4 y = 0, 1, 2, 3
- Start state: (0, 0) i.e., 4-litre and 3-litre jugs is empty initially.
- Goal state: (2, n) for any n that is 4-litre jug has 2 litres of water and 3-litre jug has any value from 0-3 since it is not specified.
- Attempting to end up in a goal state.

Production Rules: These rules are used as operators to solve the problem. They are represented as rules whose left sides are used to describe new state that result from approaching the rule.

The solution to the water-jug problem is:

Gallons in the 4-Gallon Jug	Gallons in the 3-Gallon Jug	Rule Applied
0	0	
		2
0	3	
		9
3	0	
		2
3	3	
		7
4	2	
		5 or 12
0	2	
		9 or 11
2	0	

One Solution to the Water Jug Problem

The state space for the problem can be described as a set of states, where each state represents the number of gallons in each state. The game start with the initial state described as a set of ordered pairs of integers:

- State: (x, y)
  - x = number of lts in 4 lts jug
  - y = number of lts in 3 lts jug

    x = 0, 1, 2, 3, or 4 y = 0, 1, 2, 3
- Start state: (0, 0) i.e., 4-litre and 3-litre jugs is empty initially.
- Goal state: (2, n) for any n that is 4-litre jug has 2 litres of water and 3-litre jug has any value from 0-3 since it is not specified.
- Attempting to end up in a goal state.

Production Rules: These rules are used as operators to solve the problem. They are represented as rules whose left sides are used to describe new state that result from approaching the rule.

1	(x, y) if $x < 4$	$\rightarrow (4, y)$	Fill the 4-gallon jug
2	(x, y) if $y < 3$	$\rightarrow (x, 3)$	Fill the 3-gallon jug
3	(x, y) if $x > 0$	$\rightarrow (x - d, y)$	Pour some water out of the 4-gallon jug
4	(x, y) if $y > 0$	$\rightarrow (x, y - d)$	Pour some water out of the 3-gallon jug
5	(x, y) if $x > 0$	$\rightarrow (0, y)$	Empty the 4-gallon jug on the ground
6	(x, y) if $y > 0$	$\rightarrow (x, 0)$	Empty the 3-gallon jug on the ground
7	(x, y) if $x + y \geq 4$ and $y > 0$	$\rightarrow (4, y - (4 - x))$	Pour water from the 3-gallon jug into the 4-gallon jug until the 4-gallon jug is full
8	(x, y) if $x + y \geq 3$ and $x > 0$	$\rightarrow (x - (3 - y), 3)$	Pour water from the 4-gallon jug into the 3-gallon jug until the 3-gallon jug is full
9	(x, y) if $x + y \leq 4$ and $y > 0$	$\rightarrow (x + y, 0)$	Pour all the water from the 3-gallon jug into the 4-gallon jug
10	(x, y) if $x + y \leq 3$ and $x > 0$	$\rightarrow (0, x + y)$	Pour all the water from the 4-gallon jug into the 3-gallon jug
11	$(0, 2)$	$\rightarrow (2, 0)$	Pour the 2 gallons from the 3-gallon jug into the 4-gallon jug
12	$(2, y)$	$\rightarrow (0, y)$	Empty the 2 gallons in the 4-gallon jug on the ground

Fig. 2.3 *Production Rules for the Water Jug Problem*

Chess Problem

Problem of playing chess can be defined as a problem of moving around in a state space where each state represents a legal position of the chess board.

The game start with an initial state described as an 8x8 of each position contains symbol standing for the appropriate place in the official chess opening position. A set of rules is used to move from one state to another and attempting to end up on one of a set of final states which is described as any board position in which the opponent does not have a legal move as his/her king is under attacks.

The state space representation is natural for chess. Since each state corresponds to a board position i.e. artificial well organized.

Initial State: Legal chess opening position
Goal State: Opponent does not have any legal move/king under attack

Production Rules:

These rules are used to move around the state space. They can be described easily as a set of rules consisting of two parts:

1. Left side serves as a pattern to be matching against the current board position.
2. Right side that serves decides the chess to be made to the board position to reflect the move.

To describe these rules it is convenient to introduce a notation for pattern and substitutions

E.g.:

1. `White pawn at square (file1,rank2)`

```
    Move pawn from square (file i, rank2) AND square (file i, rank2)
AND
```

2. `White pawn at square (file1,rank2)`

```
    Move pawn from square (file i, rank2) AND square (file i, rank2)
AND
```

```
    Square (file i,rank3) is empty  → To square (file i,rank4)
 AND
    Square (file i,rank4) is empty
```

2. White knight at square (file i,rank1)

```
    move Square(1,1) to  → Square(i-1,3)
  AND
    Empty Square(i-1,3)
```

3. White knight at square (1,1)

```
    move Square(1,1) to  → Square(i-1,3)
  AND
    Empty Square(i-1,3)
```

```
      Square (file i,rank3) is empty  → To square (file i,rank4)
  AND
      Square (file i,rank4) is empty

2. White knight at square (file i,rank1)
      move Square(1,1) to  → Square(i-1,3)
   AND
      Empty Square(i-1,3)
3. White knight at square (1,1)
      move Square(1,1) to  → Square(i-1,3)
   AND
      Empty Square(i-1,3)
```

8-Puzzle Problem

The **Problem** is 8-Puzzle is a square tray in which 8 square tiles are placed. The remaining 9th square is uncovered. Each tile has a number on it. A file that is adjacent to the blank space can be slide into that space. The goal is to transform the starting position into the goal position by sliding the tiles around.

Solution:

State Space: The state space for the problem can be written as a set of states where each state is position of the tiles on the tray.

Initial State: Square tray having 3x3 cells and 8 tiles number on it that are shuffled

2	8	3
1	6	4
7		5

Goal State

1	2	3
8		4
7	6	5

Production Rules: These rules are used to move from initial state to goal state. These are also defined as two parts left side pattern should match with current position and left side will be resulting position after applying the rule.

1. Tile in square (1,1)
   AND   *Move tile from square (1,1) to (2,1)*
   Empty square (2,1)

2. Tile in square (1,1)
   AND
   Empty square (1,2) *Move tile from square (1,1) to (1,2)*

3. Tile in square (2,1)
   AND
   Empty square (1,1) *Move tile from square (2,1) to (1,1)*

1,1 2	1,2 3	1,3 2
2,1 3	2,2 4	2,3 3
3,1 2	3,2 3	3,3 2

No. of Production Rules: $2 + 3 + 2 + 3 + 4 + 3 + 2 + 3 + 2 = 24$

Solution:

Travelling Salesman Problem

The **Problem** is the salesman has a list of cities, each of which he must visit exactly once. There are direct roads between each pair of cities on the list. **Find the route the salesman should follow for the shortest possible round trip that both states and finishes at any one of the cities.**

Solution:

State Space: The state space for this problem represents states in which the cities traversed by salesman and state described as salesman starting at any city in the given list of cities. A set of rules is applied such that the salesman will not traverse a city traversed once. These rules are resulted to be states with the salesman will complex the round trip and return to his starting position.

Initial State

- ➢ Salesman starting at any arbitrary city in the given list of

cities Goal State

- ➢ Visiting all cities once and only and reaching his starting state

Production rules:

These rules are used as operators to move from one state to another. Since there is a path between any pair of cities in the city list, we write the production rules for this problem as

- `Visited(city[i]) AND Not Visited(city[j])`
  - `Traverse(city[i],city[j])`
- `Visited(city[i],city[j]) AND Not Visited(city[k])`
  - `Traverse(city[j],city[k])`
- `Visited(city[j],city[i]) AND Not Visited(city[k])`
  - `Traverse(city[i],city[k])`
- `Visited(city[i],city[j],city[k]) AND Not Visited(Nil)`
  - `Traverse(city[k],city[i])`

Towers of Hanoi Problem

Problem is the state space for the problem can be described as each state representing position of the disk on each pole the position can be treated as a stack the length of the stack will be equal to maximum number of disks each post can handle. The initial state of the problem will be any one of the posts will the certain the number of disks and the other two will be empty.

Initial State:

- ➢ Full(T1) | Empty(T2) | Empty(T3)

Goal State:

- ➢ Empty(T1) | Full(T2) | Empty (T3)

Production Rules:

These are rules used to reach the Goal State. These rules use the following operations:

- POP(x) → Remove top element x from the stack and update top
- PUSH(x,y) → Push an element x into the stack and update top. [Push an element x on to the y]

Now to solve the problem the production rules can be described as follows:

1. Top(T1)<Top(T2) → PUSH(POP(T1),T2)
2. Top(T2)<Top(T1) → PUSH(POP(T2),T1)
3. Top(T1)<Top(T3) → PUSH(POP(T1),T3)
4. Top(T3)<Top(T1) → PUSH(POP(T3),T1)
5. Top(T2)<Top(T3) → PUSH(POP(T2),T3)
6. Top(T3)<Top(T2) → PUSH(POP(T3),T2)
7. Empty(T1) → PUSH(POP(T2),T1)

8. Empty(T1) → PUSH(POP(T3),T1)
9. Empty(T2) → PUSH(POP(T1),T3)
10. Empty(T3) → PUSH(POP(T1),T3)
11. Empty(T2) → PUSH(POP(T3),T2)
12. Empty(T3) → PUSH(POP(T2),T3)

Solution: Example: 3 Disks, 3 Towers

1) T1→T2
2) T1→T3
3) T2→T3
4) T1→T2
5) T3→T1
6) T3→T2
7) T1→T2

Monkey and Bananas Problem

Problem: A hungry monkey finds himself in a room in which a branch of bananas is hanging from the ceiling. The monkey unfortunately cannot reach the bananas however in the room there are also a chair and a stick. The ceiling is just right high so that a monkey standing on a chair could knock the bananas down with the stick. The monkey knows how to move round, carry other things around reach for the bananas and wave the stick in the air. **What is the best sequence of actions for the monkey to acquire lunch?**

Solution: The state space for this problem is a set of states representing the position of the monkey, position of chair, position of the stick and two flags whether monkey on the chair & whether monkey holds the stick so there is a 5-tuple representation. (M, C, S, F1, F2)

- M: position of the monkey
- C: position of the chair
- S: position of the stick
- F1: 0 or 1 depends on the monkey on the chair or not
- F2: 0 or 1 depends on the monkey holding the stick or not

Initial State (M, C, S, 0, 0)

- The objects are at different places and obviously monkey is not on the chair and not holding the stick

Goal State (G, G, G, 1, 1)

- G is the position under bananas and all objects are under it, monkey is on the chair and holding stick

Production Rules:

These are the rules which have a path for searching the goal state here we assume that when monkey hold a stick then it will swing it this assumption is necessary to simplify the representation.

Some of the production rules are:

1) (M,C,S,0,0) → (A,C,S,0,0) {An arbitrary position A}
2) (M,C,S,0,0) → (C,C,S,0,0) {monkey moves to chair position}
3) (M,C,S,0,0) → (S,S,S,0,0) {monkey brings chair to stick position}
4) (C,C,S,0,0) → (A,A,S,0,0) {push the chair to arbitrary position A}
5) (S,C,S,0,0) → (A,C,A,0,1) {Taking the stick to arbitrary position}
6) (S,C,S,0,0) → (C,C,S,0,0) {monkey moves from stick position to chair position}
7) (C,C,C,0,1) → (C,C,C,1,1)
    - {monkey and stick at the chair position, monkey on the chair and holding stick}
8) (S,C,S,0,1) → (C,C,C,0,1)

Solution:

1) (M,C,S,0,0)
2) (C,C,S,0,0)
3) (G,G,S,0,0)
4) (S,G,S,0,0)
5) (G,G,G,0,0)
6) (G,G,G,0,1)
7) (G,G,G,1,1)

Missionaries and Cannibals Problem

Problem is 3 missionaries and 3 cannibals find themselves one side of the river. They have agreed that they would like to get the other side. But the missionaries are not sure what else the cannibals have agreed to. So the missionaries want to manage the trip across the river on either side of the river is never less than the number of cannibals who are on the same side. The only boat available holds only two people at a time. How can everyone get across without missionaries risking hang eager?

Solution:
The state space for the problem contains a set of states which represent the present number of cannibals and missionaries on the either side of the bank of the river. (C,M,C1,M1,B)

- C and M are number of cannibals and missionaries on the starting bank
- C1 and M1 are number of cannibals and missionaries on the destination bank
- B is the position of the boat wither left bank (L) or right bank (R)

Initial State → C=3,M=3,B=L so (3,3,0,0,L)
Goal State → C1=3, M1=3, B=R so (0,0,3,3,R)

Production System: These are the operations used to move from one state to other state. Since at any bank the number of cannibals must less than or equal to missionaries we can write two production rules for this problem as follows:

- (C,M,C1,M1,L / C=3, M=3) → (C-2,M,C1+2,M1,R)
- (C,M,C1,M1,L / C=3, M=3) → (C-1,M-1,C1+1,M1+1,R)
- (C,M,C1,M1,L / C=3, M=3) → (C-1,M,C1+1,M1,R)
- (C,M,C1,M1,R / C=1, M=3) → (C+1,M,C1-1,M1,L)
- (C,M,C1,M1,R / C=0, M=3,C1=3,M1=0) → (C+1,M,C1-1,M1,L)

The solution path is

LEFT BANK			RIGHT BANK	
C	M	BOAT POSITION	C1	M1
3	3		0	0
1	3	→	2	0
2	3	←	1	0
0	3	→	3	0
1	3	←	2	0
1	1	→	2	2
2	2	←	1	1
2	0	→	1	3
3	0	←	0	3
1	0	→	2	3
2	0	←	1	3
0	0	→	3	3

3. Heuristic Search Techniques

Control Strategy

The question arises

> ***"How to decide which rule to apply next during the process of searching for a solution to a problem?"***

Requirements of a good search strategy:

1. It causes motion. It must reduce the difference between current state and goal state. Otherwise, it will never lead to a solution.
2. It is systematic. Otherwise, it may use more steps than necessary.
3. It is efficient. Find a good, but not necessarily the best, answer.

Breadth First Search

To solve the water jug problem systemically construct a tree with limited states as its root. Generate all the offspring and their successors from the root according to the rules until some rule produces a goal state. This process is called **Breadth-First Search.**

Algorithm:

1) Create a variable called NODE_LIST and set it to the initial state.
2) Until a goal state is found or NODE_LIST is empty do:
   a. Remove the first element from NODE_LIST and call it E. If NODE_LIST was empty quit.
   b. For each way that each rule can match the state described in E do:
      i. Apply the rule to generate a new state
      ii. If the new state is goal state, quit and return this state
      iii. Otherwise add the new state to the end of NODE_LIST

The data structure used in this algorithm is QUEUE.

Explanation of Algorithm:

- Initially put **(0,0)** state in the queue
- Apply the production rules and generate new state
- If the new states are not the goal state, (not generated before and not expanded) then only add these states to queue.

Depth First Search

There is another way of dealing the Water Jug Problem. One should construct a single branched tree utility yields a solution or until a decision terminate when the path is reaching a dead end to the previous state. If the branch is larger than the pre-specified unit then backtracking occurs to the previous state so as to create another path. This is called **Chronological Backtracking** because the order in which steps are undone depends only on the temporal sequence in which the steps were originally made. This procedure is called **Depth-First Search.**

Algorithm:

1) If the initial state is the goal state, quit return success.
2) Otherwise, do the following until success or failure is signaled
    a. Generate a successor E of the initial state, if there are no more successors, signal failure
    b. Call Depth-First Search with E as the initial state
    c. If success is returned, signal success. Otherwise continue in this loop.

The data structure used in this algorithm is STACK.
Explanation of Algorithm:

- Initially put the **(0,0)** state in the stack.
- Apply production rules and generate the new state.
- If the new states are not a goal state, (not generated before and no expanded) then only add the state to top of the Stack.
- If already generated state is encountered then POP the top of stack elements and search in another direction.

Advantages of Breadth-First Search

- BFS will not get trapped exploring a **blind alley.**
    - In case of DFS, it may follow a single path for a very long time until it has no successor.
- If there is a solution for particular problem, the BFS is generated to find it. We can find **minimal path** if there are multiple solutions for the problem.

Advantages of Depth –First Search

- DFS requires less memory since only the nodes on the current path are stored.
- Sometimes we may find the solution without examining much.

Example: Travelling Salesman Problem

To solve the TSM problem we should construct a tree which is simple, motion causing and systematic. It would explore all possible paths in the tree and return the one with the shortest length. If there are N cities, then the number of different paths among them is 1.2...(N-1) or (N-1)!

The time to examine a single path is proportional to N. So the total time required to perform this search is proportional to N!

Another strategy is, begin generating complete paths, keeping track of the shorter path so far and neglecting the paths where partial length is greater than the shortest found. This method is better than the first but it is inadequate.

To solve this efficiently we have a search called HEURISTIC SEARCH.

HEURISTIC SEARCH

Heuristic:

- It is a "rule of thumb" used to help guide search
- It is a technique that improves the efficiency of search process, possibly by sacrificing claims of completeness.
- It is involving or serving as an aid to learning, discovery, or problem-solving by experimental and especially trial-and-error methods.

Heuristic Function:

- It is a function applied to a state in a search space to indicate a likelihood of success if that state is selected
- It is a function that maps from problem state descriptions to measures of desirability usually represented by numbers
- Heuristic function is problem specific.

The purpose of heuristic function is to guide the search process in the most profitable direction by suggesting which path to follow first when more than one is available (best promising way).

We can find the TSM problem in less exponential items. On the average Heuristic improve the quality of the paths that are explored. Following procedure is to solve TRS problem

- Select a Arbitrary City as a starting city
- To select the next city, look at all cities not yet visited, and select one closest to the current city
- Repeat steps until all cities have been visited

5. Predicate Logic

Introduction

Predicate logic is used to represent Knowledge. Predicate logic will be met in Knowledge Representation Schemes and reasoning methods. There are other ways but this form is popular.

Propositional Logic

It is simple to deal with and decision procedure for it exists. We can represent real-world facts as logical propositions written as well-formed formulas.
To explore the use of predicate logic as a way of representing knowledge by looking at a specific example.

$\rightarrow$

$\rightarrow$

The above two statements becomes totally separate assertion, we would not be able to draw any conclusions about similarities between Socrates and Plato.

( )

These representations reflect the structure of the knowledge itself. These use predicates applied to arguments.

$\rightarrow$

It fails to capture the relationship between any individual being a man and that individual being a mortal.

We need variables and quantification unless we are willing to write separate statements.

Predicate:

A Predicate is a truth assignment given for a particular statement which is either true or false. To solve common sense problems by computer system, we use predicate logic.

Logic Symbols used in predicate logic

$\exists \quad - h \rightarrow -$

Predicate Logic

Terms represent specific objects in the world and can be constants, variables or functions.
Predicate Symbols refer to a particular relation among objects.
Sentences represent facts, and are made of terms, quantifiers and predicate symbols. Functions allow us to refer to objects indirectly (via some relationship).
Quantifiers and variables allow us to refer to a collection of objects without explicitly naming each object.

Some Examples

- Predicates: Brother, Sister, Mother , Father o Objects: Bill, Hillary, Chelsea, Roger
- Facts expressed as atomic sentences a.k.a. literals:
  - Father(Bill,Chelsea)
  - Mother(Hillary,Chelsea)
  - Brother(Bill,Roger)
  - Father(Bill,Chelsea)

Variables and Universal Quantification

Universal Quantification allows us to make a statement about a collection of objects:

x Cat(x) Mammel(x) : All cats are mammels

x Father(Bill,x) Mother(Hillary,x) : All of Bill's kids are also Hillary's kids.

Variables and Existential Quantification

Existential Quantification allows us to state that an object does exist (without naming it):

x Cat(x) Mean(x) : There is a mean cat.

x Father(Bill,x) Mother(Hillary,x) : There is a kid whose father is Bill and whose mother is Hillary

Nested Quantification

x,y Parent(x,y) →
Child(y,x) x y Loves(x,y)

x [Passtest(x) (x ShootDave(x))]

Functions

- Functions are terms - they refer to a specific object.
- We can use functions to symbolically refer to objects without naming them.
- Examples:

  fatherof(x) age(x) times(x,y) succ(x)
- **Using functions**
  - x Equal(x,x)
  - Equal(factorial(0),1)
  - x Equal(factorial(s(x)), times(s(x),factorial(x)))

If we use logical statements as a way of representing knowledge, then we have available a good way of reasoning with that knowledge.

Representing facts with Predicate Logic

3) All Pompeians were Romans
4) Caeser was a ruler.
5) All romans were either loyal to caeser or hated him.
6) Everyone loyal to someone.
7) People only try to assassinate rulers they are not loyal to.
8) Marcus try to assassinate Ceaser

Q. Prove that Marcus is not loyal to Ceaser by backward substitution

Representing Instance and Isa Relationships

Two attributes **isa** and **instance** play an important role in many aspects of knowledge representation. The reason for this is that they support property inheritance.

isa - used to show class inclusion, e.g. isa (mega_star,rich).

instance - used to show class membership, e.g. instance(prince,mega_star).

Pure Predicate Logic

Instance Relationship

Isa Relationship

In the figure above,

- The first five sentences of the represent the ***pure predicate logic***. In these representations, class membership is represented with unary predicates (such as Roman), each of which corresponds to a class. Asserting that P(x) is true is equivalent to asserting that x is an instance of P.
- The second part of the figure contains representations that use the ***instance*** predicate explicitly. The predicate instance is a binary one, whose first argument is an object and whose second argument is a class to which the object belongs. But these representations do not use an explicit isa predicate.
- The third part contains representations that use both the instance and ***isa*** predicates explicitly. The use of the isa predicate simplifies the representation of sentence 3, but it requires that one additional axiom be provided. This additional axiom describes how an instance relation and an isa relation can be combined to derive a new instance relation.

Computable Functions and Predicates

This is fine if the number of facts is not very large or if the facts themselves are sufficiently unstructured that there is little alternative. But suppose we want to express simple facts, such as the following greater-than and less-than relationships:

gt(1,0)	lt(0,1)
gt(2,1)	lt(1,2)
gt(3,2)	lt(2,3)

Clearly we do not want to have to write out the representation of each of these facts individually. For one thing, there are infinitely many of them. But even if we only consider the finite number of them that can be represented, say, using a single machine word per number, it would be extremely inefficient to store explicitly a large set of statements when we could, instead, so easily compute each one as we need it. Thus it becomes useful to augment our representation by these ***computable predicates.***

1. Marcus was a Man => ( )
2. Marcus was a Pompeian =>
3. Marcus born in 40 AD =>
4. All men are mortal =>
5. All Pompeians died when the volcano was erupted in 79 AD.
6. No mortal lives longer than 150 years
7. It is now 1991 =>
8. Alive means not deal
9. If someone dies then he is dead at all later times

Prove that Marcus is dead now.

Resolution:

A procedure to prove a statement, Resolution attempts to show that Negation of Statement gives Contradiction with known statements. It simplifies proof procedure by first converting the statements into canonical form. Simple iterative process; at each step, 2 clauses called the parent clauses are compared, yielding a new clause that has been inferred from them.

Resolution refutation:

Convert all sentences to CNF (conjunctive normal form)

Negate the desired conclusion (converted to CNF)

Apply resolution rule until either

- Derive false (a contradiction)
- Can't apply any more

Resolution inference rule

$$\frac{(\alpha \vee \neg\beta) \wedge (\gamma \vee \beta) \text{ premise}}{(\alpha \vee \gamma) \text{ conclusion}}$$

- If we derive a contradiction, then the conclusion follows from the axioms
- If we can't apply any more, then the conclusion cannot be proved from the axioms.

Sometimes from the collection of the statements we have, we want to know the answer of this question - "Is it possible to prove some other statements from what we actually know?" In order to prove this we need to make some inferences and those other statements can be shown true using **Refutation proof method** i.e. proof by contradiction using Resolution. So for the asked goal we will negate the goal and will add it to the given statements to prove the contradiction.

So **resolution refutation** for propositional logic is a complete **proof** procedure. So if the thing that you're trying to **prove** is, in fact, entailed by the things that you've assumed, then you can **prove** it using **resolution refutation**.

Clauses:

- Resolution can be applied to certain class of wff called clauses.
- A clause is defined as a wff consisting of disjunction of literals.

Conjunctive Normal Form or Clause Normal Form:

Clause form is an approach to Boolean logic that expresses formulas as conjunctions of clauses with an AND or OR. Each clause connected by a conjunction or AND must be wither a literal or contain a disjunction or OR operator. In clause form, a statement is a series of ORs connected by ANDs.

A statement is in conjunctive normal form if it is a conjunction (sequence of ANDs) consisting of one or more conjuncts, each of which is a disjunction (OR) of one or more literals (i.e., statement letters and negations of statement letters).

All of the following formulas in the variables A, B, C, D, and E are in conjunctive normal form:

- $\neg A \wedge (B \vee C)$
- $(A \vee B) \wedge (\neg B \vee C \vee \neg D) \wedge (D \vee \neg E)$
- $A \vee B$
- $A \wedge B$

Conversion to Clause Form:

$$\forall x : [Roman(x) \wedge know(x, Marcus)] \rightarrow$$
$$[hate(x, Caesar) \vee (\forall y : \exists z : hate(y, z) \rightarrow thinkcrazy(x, y))]$$

➔ Clause Form:

$$\neg Roman(x) \wedge \neg know(x, Marcus) \vee$$
$$hate(x, Caesar) \vee \neg hate(y, z) \vee thinkcrazy(x, z)$$

Algorithm:

1.)

2. Reduce the scope of each to a single term

3. Standardize variables so that each quantifier binds a unique variable.
4. Move all quantifiers to the left of the formulas without changing their relative order.

5. Eliminate existential quantifiers. We can eliminate the quantifier by substituting for the variable a reference to a function that produces the desired value.

   ∀x,∃y: Fatherof(y,x)=>∀x: Fatherof(S2(s),x) President(func()) → func is called a skolem function.

   In general the function must have the same number of arguments as the number of universal quantifiers in the current scope.

   Skolemize to remove existential quantifiers. This step replaces existentially quantified variables by **Skolem functions**. For example, convert (x)P(x) to P(c) where c is a brand new constant symbol that is not used in any other sentence (c is called a **Skolem constant**). More generally, if the existential quantifier is within the scope of a universal quantified variable, then introduce a Skolem function that depends on the universally quantified variable. For example, " x y P(x,y) is converted to " x P(x, f(x)). f is called a Skolem function, and must be a brand new function name that does not occur in any other part of the logic sentence.

6. Drop the prefix. At this point, all remaining variables are universally quantified.

   $[\neg Roman(x) \vee \neg know(x, Marcus)] \vee$
   $[hate(x, Caesar) \vee (\neg hate(y, z) \vee thinkcrazy(x, y))]$

7. Convert the matrix into a conjunction of disjunctions.

8. Create a separate clause corresponding to each conjunct in order for a well formed formula to be true, all the clauses that are generated from it must be true.
9. Standardize apart the variables in set of clauses generated in step 8. Rename the variables. So that no two clauses make reference to same variable.

Convert the statements to clause form

1. man(marcus)
2. pompeian(marcus)
4. ruler(caeser)
6. x, y: loyalto(x,y)
7. y: person(x) ruler(y) tryassacinate(x,y)
8. tryassacinate(marcus, caeser)

The resultant clause form is

Basis of Resolution:

Resolution process is applied to pair of parent clauses to produce a derived clause. Resolution procedure operates by taking 2 clauses that each contain the same literal. The literal must occur in the positive form in one clause and negative form in the other. The resolvent is obtained by combining all of the literals of two parent clauses except ones that cancel. If the clause that is produced in an empty clause, then a contradiction has been found.

Eg: winter and winter will produce the empty clause.

If a contradiction exists, then eventually it will be found. Of course, if no contradiction exists, it is possible that the procedure will never terminate, although as we will see, there are often ways of detecting that no contradiction exists.

Resolution in Propositional Logic:

Example: Consider the following axioms

P (P Q) →R (S T) → Q T

prove that R is true

→ .Hence, R is true.

Unification Algorithm

In propositional logic it is easy to determine that two literals cannot both be true at the same time.

Simply look for L and ~L . In predicate logic, this matching process is more complicated, since bindings of variables must be considered.

In order to determine contradictions we need a matching procedure that compares two literals and discovers whether there exist a set of substitutions that makes them identical.

There is a recursive procedure that does this matching. It is called Unification algorithm.

The process of finding a substitution for predicate parameters is called **unification.**

We need to know:

- that 2 literals can be matched.
- the substitution is that makes the literals identical.

There is a simple algorithm called the unification algorithm that does this.

The Unification Algorithm

1. Initial predicate symbols must match.
2. For each pair of predicate arguments:
   - Different constants cannot match.
   - A variable may be replaced by a constant.
   - A variable may be replaced by another variable.
   - A variable may be replaced by a function as long as the function does not contain an instance of the variable.

- When attempting to match 2 literals, all substitutions must be made to the entire literal.
- There may be many substitutions that unify 2 literals; the most general unifier is always desired.

Unification Example:

(,) (()) () h ((,h (,): ():) (/)(/)→ ( )) ! h ():((,) /, ,h /) h (,)

(h (),) (,) (,)

The object of the Unification procedure is to discover at least one substitution that causes two literals to match. Usually, if there is one such substitution there are many

could be unified with any of the following substitutions:

In Unification algorithm each literal is represented as a list, where first element is the name of a predicate and the remaining elements are arguments. The argument may be a single element (atom) or may be another list.

The unification algorithm recursively matches pairs of elements, one pair at a time. The matching rules are:

- Different constants, functions or predicates cannot match, whereas identical ones can.
- A variable can match another variable, any constant or a function or predicate expression, subject to the condition that the function or [predicate expression must not contain any instance of the variable being matched (otherwise it will lead to infinite recursion).
- The substitution must be consistent. Substituting y for x now and then z for x later is inconsistent. (a substitution y for x written as y/x)

Algorithm: Unify(Ll, L2)

1. If *L1* or *L2* are both variables or constants, then:
   (a) If *L1* and *L2* are identical, then return NIL.
   (b) Else if *L1* is a variable, then if *L1* occurs in *L2* then return {FAIL}, else return (*L2/L1*).
   (c) Else if *L2* is a variable then if *L2* occurs in *L1* then return {FAIL}, else return (*L1/L2*).
   (d) Else return {FAIL}.
2. If the initial predicate symbols in *L1* and *L2* are not identical, then return {FAIL}.
3. If *LI* and *L2* have a different number of arguments, then return {FAIL}.
4. Set *SUBST* to NIL. (At the end of this procedure, *SUBST* will contain all the substitutions used to unify *L1* and *L2*.)
5. For *i* ← 1 to number of arguments in *L1*:
   (a) Call Unify with the *i*th argument of *L1* and the *i*th argument of *L2*, putting result in *S*.
   (b) If *S* contains FAIL then return {FAIL}.
   (c) If *S* is not equal to NIL then:
      (i) Apply *S* to the remainder of both *L1* and *L2*.
      (ii) *SUBST* : = APPEND(S, *SUBST*).
6. Return *SUBST*.

Example:

Suppose we want to unify *p(X,Y,Y)* with *p(a,Z,b)*.
Initially *E* is *{p(X,Y,Y)=p(a,Z,b)}*.
The first time through the while loop, *E* becomes *{X=a,Y=Z,Y=b}*.
Suppose *X=a* is selected next.
Then *S* becomes*{X/a}* and *E* becomes *{Y=Z,Y=b}*.
Suppose *Y=Z* is selected.
Then *Y* is replaced by *Z* in *S* and *E*.
S becomes*{X/a,Y/Z}* and *E* becomes *{Z=b}*.
Finally *Z=b* is selected, *Z* is replaced by *b*, *S* becomes *{X/a,Y/b,Z/b}*, and *E* becomes empty.
The substitution *{X/a,Y/b,Z/b}* is returned as an MGU.

Unification:

((h,), (h,))={ /}

Resolution in Predicate Logic

- Two literals are contradictory if one can be unified with the negation of the other.
    - For example man(x) and man (Himalayas) are contradictory since man(x) and man(Himalayas) can be unified.
- In predicate logic unification algorithm is used to locate pairs of literals that cancel out.
- It is important that if two instances of the same variable occur, then they must be given identical substitutions

Algorithm: Resolution

1. Convert all the statements of F to clause form.
2. Negate P and convert the result to clause form. Add it to the set of clauses obtained in 1.
3. Repeat until either a contradiction is found, no progress can be made, or a prede- termined amount of effort has been expended.
   (a) Select two clauses. Call these the parent clauses.
   (b) Resolve them together. The resolvent will be the disjunction of all the literals of both parent clauses with appropriate substitutions performed and with the following exception: If there is one pair of literals $T1$ and $\neg T2$ such that one of the parent clauses contains $T2$ and the other contains $T1$ and if $T1$ and $T2$ are unifiable, then neither $T1$ nor $T2$ should appear in the resolvent. We call $T1$ and $T2$ *Complementary literals*. Use the substitution produced by the unification to create the resolvent. If there is more than one pair of complementary literals, only one pair should be omitted from the resolvent.
   (c) If the resolvent is the empty clause, then a contradiction has been found. If it is not, then add it to the set of clauses available to the procedure.

Prove that Marcus hates ceaser using resolution.

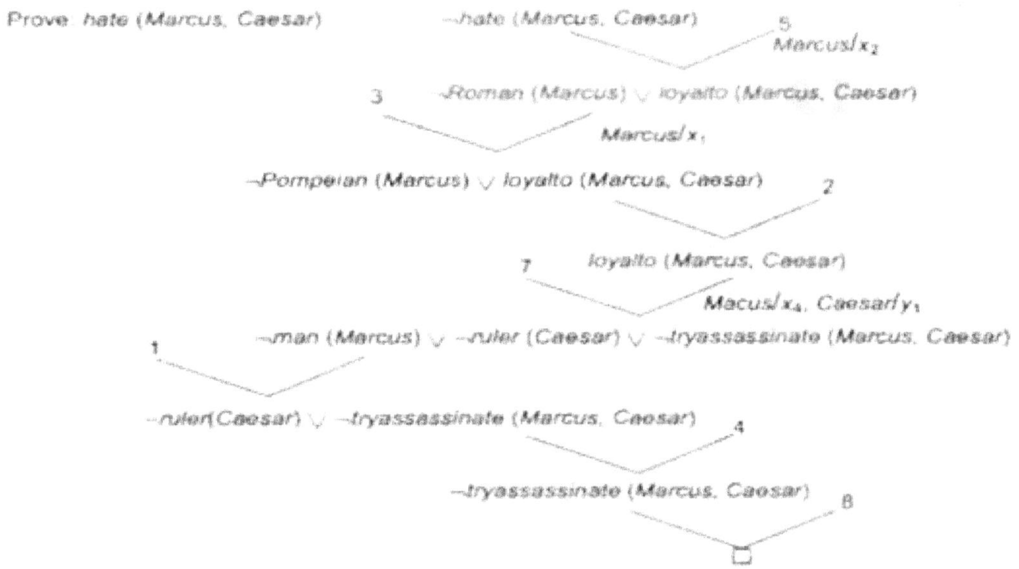

Example:

John likes all kinds of food.
Apples are food.
Chicken is food.
Anything anyone eats and it is not killed is food.
Bill eats peanuts and is still alive.
Swe eats everything bill eats

(a) Convert all the above statements into predicate logic
(b) Show that John likes peanuts using back chaining
(c) Convert the statements into clause form
(d) Using Resolution show that "John likes peanuts"

Answer:

(a) Predicate Logic:

1.
2.
3.

5.
6.

(b) Backward Chaining Proof:

(c) Clause Form:

1.
2.
3.
4.
5.
6.
7.

(d) Resolution Proof:

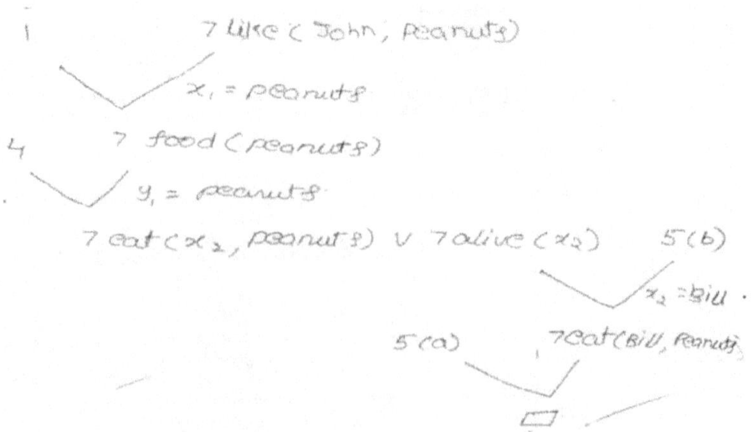

Answering Questions

We can also use the proof procedure to answer questions such as "who tried to assassinate Caesar" by proving:

- Tryassassinate(y,Caesar).
- Once the proof is complete we need to find out what was substitution was made for y.

We show how resolution can be used to answer fill-in-the-blank questions, such as "When did Marcus die?" or "Who tried to assassinate a ruler?" Answering these questions involves finding a known statement that matches the terms given in the question and then responding with another piece of the same statement that fills the slot demanded by the question.

From Clause Form to Horn Clauses

The operation is to convert Clause form to Horn Clauses. This operation is not always possible. Horn clauses are clauses in normal form that have one or zero positive literals. The conversion from a clause in normal form with one or zero positive literals to a Horn clause is done by using the implication property.

→

Example:

Predicate

∀x (¬literate(x) ⊃ (¬writes(x) ∧ ¬∃y(reads(x,y) ∧ book(y))))

Simplify

∀x (literate(x) ∨ (¬writes(x) ∧ ¬∃y(reads(x,y) ∧ book(y))))

Move negations in

∀x (literate(x) ∨ (¬writes(x) ∧ ∀y(¬(reads(x,y) ∧ book(y)))))

∀x (literate(x) ∨ (¬writes(x) ∧ ∀y(¬reads(x,y) ∨ ¬book(y))))

No Skolemize (there are no existential quantifiers)

Remove universal quantifier

∀x ∀y (literate(x) ∨ (¬writes(x) ∧ (¬reads(x,y) ∨ ¬book(y))))

literate(x) ∨ (¬writes(x) ∧ (¬reads(x,y) ∨ ¬book(y)))

Distribute disjunctions

(literate(x) ∨ ¬writes(x)) ∧ (literate(x) ∨ ¬reads(x,y) ∨ ¬book(y))

(¬writes(x) ∨ literate(x)) ∧ (¬reads(x,y) ∨ ¬book(y) ∨ literate(x))

Convert to Clause Normal Form

¬writes(x) ∨ literate(x)

¬reads(x,y) ∨ ¬book(y) ∨ literate(x)

Convert to Horn Clauses

writes(x) ⊃ literate(x)

reads(x,y) ∧ book(y) ⊃ literate(x)

Example 2

Predicate
$\forall x\,(\text{literate}(x) \supset \text{reads}(x) \vee \text{write}(x))$

Simplify
$\forall x\,(\neg\text{literate}(x) \vee \text{reads}(x) \vee \text{write}(x))$

The negations are already in
$\forall x\,(\neg\text{literate}(x) \vee \text{reads}(x) \vee \text{write}(x))$

No Skolemize (there are no existential quantifiers)

Remove universal quantifier
$\neg\text{literate}(x) \vee \text{reads}(x) \vee \text{write}(x)$

No disjunctions

It is already a Clause Normal Form
$\neg\text{literate}(x) \vee \text{reads}(x) \vee \text{write}(x)$

It is not possible to convert to Horn Clauses because there are two positive literals ($\text{reads}(x)$ and $\text{write}(x)$).

4. Knowledge Representation Issues

Introduction:

Knowledge plays an important role in AI systems. The kinds of knowledge might need to be represented in AI systems:

- **Objects:** Facts about objects in our world domain. e.g. Guitars have strings, trumpets are brass instruments.
- **Events:** Actions that occur in our world. e.g. Steve Vai played the guitar in Frank Zappa's Band.
- **Performance:** A behavior like playing the guitar involves knowledge about how to do things.
- **Meta-knowledge:** Knowledge about what we know. e.g. Bobrow's Robot who plan's a trip. It knows that it can read street signs along the way to find out where it is.

Representations & Mappings:

In order to solve complex problems in AI we need:

- A large amount of knowledge
- Some mechanisms for manipulating that knowledge to create solutions to new problem.

A variety of ways of representing knowledge have been exploited in AI problems. In this regard we deal with two different kinds of entities:

- **Facts:** truths about the real world and these are the things we want to represent.
- **Representation of the facts** in some chosen formalism. These are the things which we will actually be able to manipulate.

One way to think of structuring these entities is as two levels:

Knowledge Level, at which facts are described.

Symbol Level, at which representations of objects at the knowledge level are defined in terms of symbols that can be manipulated by programs.

Mappings between Facts and Representations:

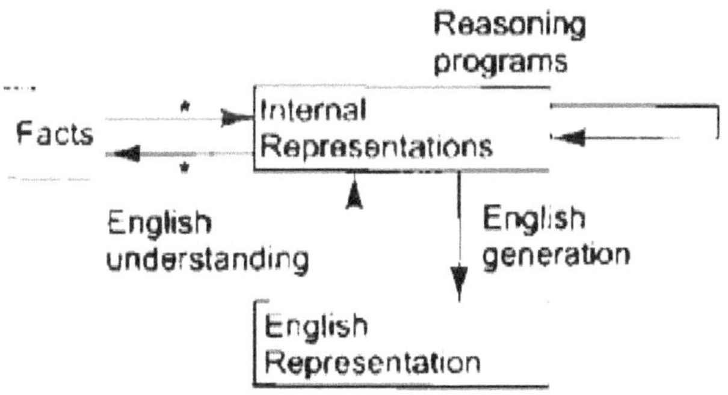

The model in the above figure focuses on facts, representations and on the 2-way mappings that must exist between them. These links are called *Representation Mappings.*

- Forward Representation mappings maps from Facts to Representations.
- Backward Representation mappings maps from Representations to Facts.

English or natural language is an obvious way of representing and handling facts. Regardless of representation for facts, we use in program, we need to be concerned with English Representation of those facts in order to facilitate getting information into or out of the system.

Mapping functions from English Sentences to Representations: Mathematical logic as representational formalism.

Example:

The fact represented by that English sentence can also be represented in logic as:

Suppose that we also have a logical representation of the fact that

Then, using the deductive mechanisms of logic, we may generate the new

Using an appropriate backward mapping function the English sentence "Spot has a tail" can be generated.

Fact-Representation mapping may not be one-to-one but rather are many-to-many which are a characteristic of English Representation. Good Representation can make a reasoning program simple.

Example:

From the two statements we can conclude that "Each dog has a tail." From the statement 1, we conclude that "Each dog has more than one tail."

When we try to convert English sentence into some other represent such as logical propositions, we first decode what facts the sentences represent and then convert those facts into the new representations. When an AI program manipulates the internal representation of facts these new representations should also be interpretable as new representations of facts.

Mutilated Checkerboard Problem:

Problem: In a normal chess board the opposite corner squares have been eliminated. The given task is to cover all the squares on the remaining board by dominoes so that each domino covers two squares. No overlapping of dominoes is allowed, can it be done? Consider three data structures

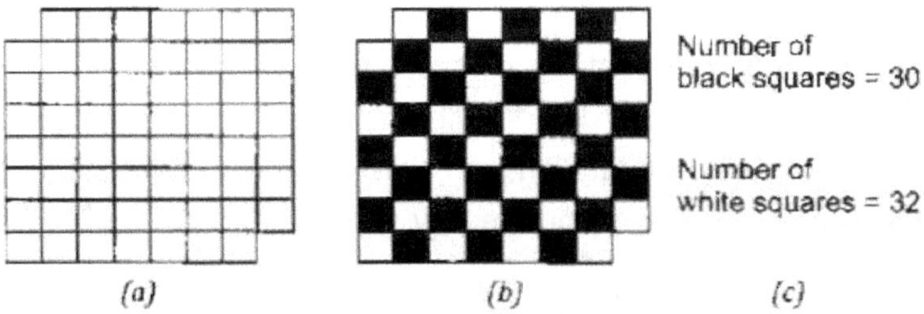

Three Representations of a Mutilated Checker board

The first representation does not directly suggest the answer to the problem. The second may suggest. The third representation does, when combined with the single additional facts that each domino must cover exactly one white square and one black square.

The puzzle is impossible to complete. A domino placed on the chessboard will always cover one white square and one black square. Therefore a collection of dominoes placed on the board will cover an equal numbers of squares of each color. If the two white corners are removed from the board then 30 white squares and 32 black squares remain to be covered by dominoes, so this is impossible. If the two black corners are removed instead, then 32 white squares and 30 black squares remain, so it is again impossible.

The solution is number of squares must be equal for positive solution.

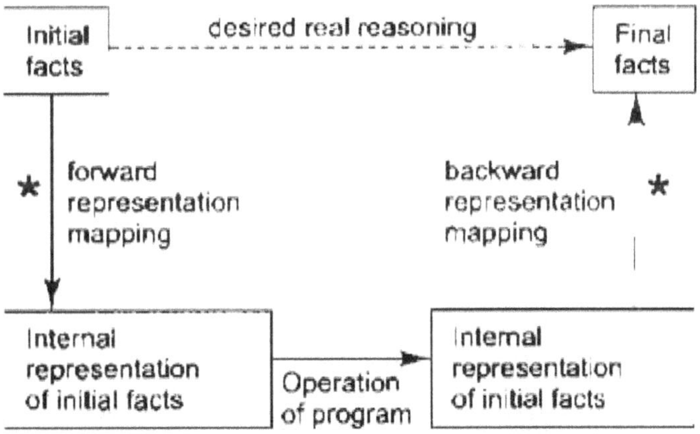

Representation of Facts

In the above figure, the dotted line across the top represents the abstract reasoning process that a program is intended to model. The solid line across the bottom represents the concrete reasoning process that a particular program performs. This program successfully models the abstract process to the extent that, when the backward representation mapping is applied to the program's output, the appropriate final facts are actually generated.

If no good mapping can be defined for a problem, then no matter how good the program to solve the problem is, it will not be able to produce answers that correspond to real answers to the problem.

Using Knowledge

Let us consider to what applications and how knowledge may be used.

- **Learning:** acquiring knowledge. This is more than simply adding new facts to a knowledge base. New data may have to be classified prior to storage for easy retrieval, etc.. Interaction and inference with existing facts to avoid redundancy and replication in the knowledge and also so that facts can be updated.
- **Retrieval:** The representation scheme used can have a critical effect on the efficiency of the method. Humans are very good at it. Many AI methods have tried to model human.
- **Reasoning:** Infer facts from existing data.

If a system on only knows:

- Miles Davis is a Jazz Musician.
- All Jazz Musicians can play their instruments well.

If things like *Is Miles Davis a Jazz Musician?* or *Can Jazz Musicians play their instruments well?* are asked then the answer is readily obtained from the data structures and procedures.

However a question like "*Can Miles Davis play his instrument well?*" requires reasoning. The above are all related. For example, it is fairly obvious that learning and reasoning involve retrieval etc.

Approaches to Knowledge Representation

A good Knowledge representation enables fast and accurate access to Knowledge and understanding of content. ***The goal of Knowledge Representation (KR) is to facilitate conclusions from knowledge.***

The following properties should be possessed by a knowledge representation system.

- **Representational Adequacy:** the ability to represent all kinds of knowledge that are needed in that domain;
- **Inferential Adequacy:** the ability to manipulate the knowledge represented to produce new knowledge corresponding to that inferred from the original;
- **Inferential Efficiency:** the ability to incorporate into the knowledge structure additional information that can be used to focus the attention of the inference mechanisms in the most promising directions.
- **Acquisitional Efficiency:** the ability to acquire new information easily. The simplest case involves direct insertion, by a person of new knowledge into the database. Ideally, the program itself would be able to control knowledge acquisition.

No single system that optimizes all of the capabilities for all kinds of knowledge has yet been found. As a result, multiple techniques for knowledge representation exist.

Knowledge Representation Schemes

There are four types of Knowledge Representation:

- **Relational Knowledge:**
  - provides a framework to compare two objects based on equivalent attributes
  - any instance in which two different objects are compared is a relational type of knowledge

- **Inheritable Knowledge:**
  - is obtained from associated objects
  - it prescribes a structure in which new objects are created which may inherit all or a subset of attributes from existing objects.
- **Inferential Knowledge**
  - is inferred from objects through relations among objects
  - Example: a word alone is simple syntax, but with the help of other words in phrase the reader may infer more from a word; this inference within linguistic is called semantics.
- **Declarative Knowledge**
  - a statement in which knowledge is specified, but the use to which that knowledge is to be put is not given.
  - Example: laws, people's name; there are facts which can stand alone, not dependent on other knowledge

Procedural Knowledge
  - a representation in which the control information, to use the knowledge is embedded in the knowledge itself.
  - Example: computer programs, directions and recipes; these indicate specific use or implementation

Simple relational knowledge

The simplest way of storing facts is to use a relational method where each fact about a set of objects is set out systematically in columns. This representation gives little opportunity for inference, but it can be used as the knowledge basis for inference engines.

- Simple way to store facts.
- Each fact about a set of objects is set out systematically in columns.
- Little opportunity for inference.
- Knowledge basis for inference engines.

Table - Simple Relational Knowledge

Player	Height	Weight	Bats - Throws
Aaron	6-0	180	Right - Right
Mays	5-10	170	Right - Right
Ruth	6-2	215	Left - Left
Williams	6-3	205	Left - Right

Given the facts it is not possible to answer simple question such as "Who is the heaviest player?" but if a procedure for finding heaviest player is provided, then these facts will enable that procedure to compute an answer. We can ask things like who "bats - left" and "throws - right".

Inheritable Knowledge

Here the knowledge elements inherit attributes from their parents. The knowledge is embodied in the design hierarchies found in the functional, physical and process domains. Within the hierarchy, elements inherit attributes from their parents, but in many cases not all attributes of the parent elements be prescribed to the child elements.

The inheritance is a powerful form of inference, but not adequate. The basic KR needs to be augmented with inference mechanism.

The KR in hierarchical structure, shown below, is called "semantic network" or a collection of "frames" or "slot-and-filler structure". The structure shows property inheritance and way for insertion of additional knowledge.

Property inheritance: The objects or elements of specific classes inherit attributes and values from more general classes. The classes are organized in a generalized hierarchy.

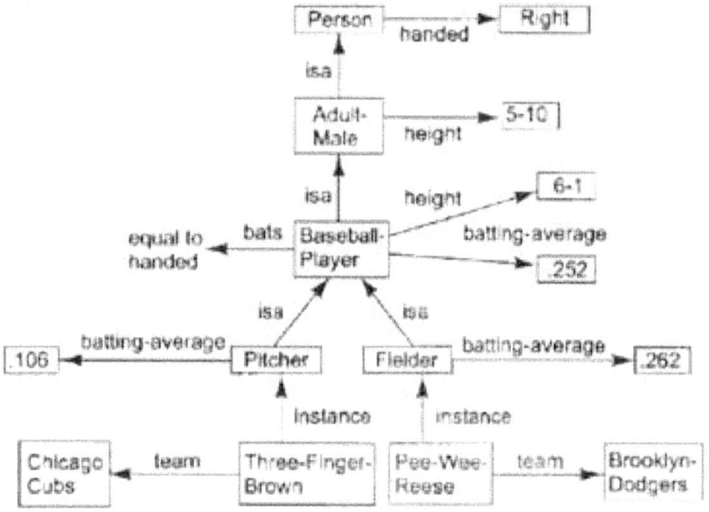

Inheritable Knowledge

Baseball Knowledge
- isa: show class inclusion
- instance: show class membership

The directed arrows represent attributes (isa, instance, team) originates at object being described and terminates at object or its value.

The box nodes represent objects and values of the attributes.

Viewing a node as a frame

Example: Baseball-player

Isa:	Adult-Male
Bats:	EQUAL handed
Height:	6-1
Batting-average:	0.252

Algorithm: Property Inheritance

To retrieve a value *V* for attribute A of an instance object *O*:

1. Find *O* in the knowledge base.
2. If there is a value there for the attribute A, report that value.
3. Otherwise, see if there is a value for the attribute *instance*. If not, then fail.
4. Otherwise, move to the node corresponding to that value and look for a value for the attribute *A*. If one is found, report it.
5. Otherwise, do until there is no value for the *isa* attribute or until an answer is found:
   (a) Get the value of the *isa* attribute and move to that node.
   (b) See if there is a value for the attribute *A*. If there is, report it.

This algorithm is simple. It describes the basic mechanism of inheritance. It does not say what to do if there is more than one value of the instance or "isa" attribute.

This can be applied to the example of knowledge base, to derive answers to the following queries:

- team (Pee-Wee-Reese) = Brooklyn-Dodger
- batting-average (Three-Finger-Brown) = 0.106
- height (Pee-Wee-Reese) = 6.1
- bats (Three-Finger-Brown) = right

Inferential Knowledge:

This knowledge generates new information from the given information. This new information does not require further data gathering from source, but does require analysis of the given information to generate new knowledge. In this, we represent knowledge as formal logic.

Example:

- given a set of relations and values, one may infer other values or relations
- a predicate logic (a mathematical deduction) is used to infer from a set of attributes.
- inference through predicate logic uses a set of logical operations to relate individual data.
- the symbols used for the logic operations are:

" → " **(implication)**, " ¬ " **(not)**, " V " **(or)**, " Λ " **(and)**,
" ∀ " **(for all)**, " ∃ " **(there exists)**.

Examples of predicate logic statements :

1. "*Wonder*" is a name of a dog : **dog (wonder)**
2. All dogs belong to the class of animals : **∀ x : dog (x) → animal(x)**
3. All animals either live on land or in water : **∀ x : animal(x) → live (x, land) V live (x, water)**

From these three statements we can infer that :

" ***Wonder*** **lives either on land or on water.**"

Note : If more information is made available about these objects and their relations, then more knowledge can be inferred.

Procedural Knowledge

Procedural knowledge can be represented in programs in many ways. The most common way is simply as for doing something. The machine uses the knowledge when it executes the code to perform a task. Procedural Knowledge is the knowledge encoded in some procedures.

Unfortunately, this way of representing procedural knowledge gets low scores with respect to the properties of inferential adequacy (because it is very difficult to write a program that can reason about another program's behavior) and acquisitional efficiency (because the process of updating and debugging large pieces of code becomes unwieldy).

The most commonly used technique for representing procedural knowledge in AI programs is the use of production rules.

If: ninth inning, and
score is close, and
less than 2 outs, and
first base is vacant, and
batter is better hitter than next batter,
Then: walk the batter.

Procedural Knowledge as Rules

Production rules, particularly ones that are augmented with information on how they are to be used, are more procedural than are the other representation methods. But making a clean distinction between declarative and procedural knowledge is difficult. The important difference is in how the knowledge is used by the procedures that manipulate it.

Heuristic or Domain Specific knowledge can be represented using Procedural Knowledge.

Issues in Knowledge Representation

Below are listed issues that should be raised when using knowledge representation techniques:

- Important Attributes :

  Any attribute of objects so basic that they occur in almost every problem domain ?

- Relationship among attributes:

  Any important relationship that exists among object attributes ?

- Choosing Granularity :

  At what level of detail should the knowledge be represented ?

- Set of objects :

  How sets of objects be represented ?

- Finding Right structure :

  Given a large amount of knowledge stored, how can relevant parts be accessed ?

Important Attributes : *(Ref. Example - Fig. Inheritable KR)*

There are attributes that are of general significance.

There are two attributes **"instance"** and **"isa"**, that are of general importance. These attributes are important because they support *property inheritance*.

The attributes are called a variety of things in AI systems, but the names do not matter. What does matter is that they represent class membership and class inclusion and that class inclusion is transitive. The predicates are used in Logic Based Systems.

Relationship among Attributes

- The attributes to describe objects are themselves entities that we represent.
- The relationship between the attributes of an object, independent of specific knowledge they encode, may hold properties like:
  - *Inverses, existence in an isa hierachy, techniques for reasoning about values and single valued attributes.*

Inverses :

This is about *consistency check*, while a value is added to one attribute. The entities are related to each other in many different ways. The figure shows attributes *(isa, instance, and team)*, each with a directed arrow, originating at the object being described and terminating either at the object or its value.

There are two ways of realizing this:

- first, represent two relationships in a *single representation*; e.g., a logical representation, ***team(Pee-Wee-Reese, Brooklyn–Dodgers)***, that can be interpreted as a statement about Pee-Wee-Reese or Brooklyn–Dodger.
- second, use attributes that focus on a *single entity but use them in pairs*, one the inverse of the other; for e.g., one, ***team = Brooklyn–Dodgers*** , and the other, ***team = Pee-Wee-Reese, ...***

The second way can be realized using semantic net and frame based systems. This Inverses is used in Knowledge Acquisition Tools.

Existence in an "isa" hierarchy :

This is about *generalization-specialization*, like, classes of objects and specialized subsets of those classes. There are attributes and specialization of attributes.

Example: the attribute *"height"* is a specialization of general attribute *"physical-size"* which is, in turn, a specialization of *"physical-attribute"*. These generalization-specialization relationships for attributes are important because they support inheritance.

This also provides information about constraints on the values that the attribute can have and mechanisms for computing those values.

Techniques for reasoning about values :

This is about *reasoning values of attributes* not given explicitly.

Several kinds of information are used in reasoning, like,

height : must be in a unit of length,

age : of person can not be greater than the age of person's parents.

The values are often specified when a knowledge base is created.

Several kinds of information can play a role in this reasoning, including:

Information about the type of the value.

Constraints on the value often stated in terms of related entities.

Rules for computing the value when it is needed. (Example: of such a rule in for bats attribute). These rules are called **backward rules.** Such rules have also been called **if-needed rules.**

Rules that describe actions that should be taken if a value ever becomes known. These rules are called **forward rules**, or sometimes **if-added rules**.

Single valued attributes :

This is about a *specific attribute* that is guaranteed to take a unique value.

Example : A baseball player can at time have only a single height and be a member of only one team. KR systems take different approaches to provide support for single valued attributes.

- Introduce an explicit notation for temporal interval. If two different values are ever asserted for the same temporal interval, signal a contradiction automatically.
- Assume that the only temporal interval that is of interest is now. So if a new value is asserted, replace the old value.
- Provide no explicit support. Logic-based systems are in this category. But in these systems, knowledge base builders can add axioms that state that if an attribute has one value then it is known not to have all other values.

Choosing Granularity

What level should the knowledge be represented and what are the primitives ?

- Should there be a small number or should there be a large number of low-level primitives or High-level facts.
- High-level facts may not be adequate for inference while Low-level primitives may require a lot of storage.

Example of Granularity :

- Suppose we are interested in following facts

  John spotted Sue.
- This could be represented as

  Spotted (agent(John), object (Sue))
- Such a representation would make it easy to answer questions such are

  Who spotted Sue ?
- Suppose we want to know

  Did John see Sue ?
- Given only one fact, we cannot discover that answer.
- We can add other facts, such as

  Spotted (x , y) → saw (x , y)
- We can now infer the answer to the question.

Choosing the Granularity of Representation Primitives are fundamental concepts such as holding, seeing, playing and as English is a very rich language with over half a million words it is clear we will find difficulty in deciding upon which words to choose as our primitives in a series of situations. Separate levels of understanding require different levels of primitives and these need many rules to link together similar primitives.

Set of Objects

Certain properties of objects that are true as member of a set but not as individual;

Example : Consider the assertion made in the sentences

"there are more *sheep* than *people* in Australia", and

"*English* speakers can be found all over the world."

To describe these facts, the only way is to attach assertion to the sets representing people, sheep, and English.

The reason to represent sets of objects is :

If a property is true for all or most elements of a set,

then it is more efficient to associate it once with the set

rather than to associate it explicitly with every elements of the set .

This is done in different ways :

- in logical representation through the use of *universal quantifier*, and
- in hierarchical structure where node represent sets, the *inheritance propagate* set level assertion down to individual.

Example: assert **large (elephant)**;

Remember to make clear distinction between,

- whether we are asserting some property of the set itself, means, **the set of elephants is large,** or
- asserting some property that holds for individual elements of the set , means, **any thing that is an elephant is large**.

There are three ways in which sets may be represented :

(a) Name, as in the example - Ref Fig. Inheritable KR, the node - Baseball-Player and the predicates as Ball and Batter in logical representation.

(b) Extensional definition is to list the numbers, and

(c) In tensional definition is to provide a rule, that returns true or false depending on whether the object is in the set or not.

Finding Right Structure

Access to right structure for describing a particular situation.

It requires, selecting an initial structure and then revising the choice.
While doing so, it is necessary to solve following problems :

- how to perform an initial selection of the most appropriate structure.
- how to fill in appropriate details from the current situations.
- how to find a better structure if the one chosen initially turns out not to be appropriate.
- what to do if none of the available structures is appropriate.
- when to create and remember a new structure.

There is no good, general purpose method for solving all these problems.
Some knowledge representation techniques solve some of them.

6. Representing Knowledge using Rules

Procedural versus Declaration Knowledge

Declarative Knowledge	**Procedural Knowledge**
Factual information stored in memory and known to be static in nature.	the knowledge of how to perform, or how to operate
knowledge of facts or concepts	a skill or action that you are capable of performing
knowledge about that something true or false	Knowledge about how to do something to reach a particular objective or goal
knowledge is specified but how to use to which that knowledge is to be put is not given	control information i.e., necessary to use the knowledge is considered to be embedded in the knowledge itself
E.g.: concepts, facts, propositions, assertions, semantic nets ...	E.g.: procedures, rules, strategies, agendas, models
It is explicit knowledge (describing)	It is tacit knowledge (doing)

The **declarative representation** is one in which the knowledge is specified but how to use to which that knowledge is to be put is not given.

Declarative knowledge answers the question 'What do you know?'

It is your understanding of things, ideas, or concepts.

In other words, declarative knowledge can be thought of as the who, what, when, and where of information.

Declarative knowledge is normally discussed using nouns, like the names of people, places, or things or dates that events occurred.

The **procedural representation** is one in which the control information i.e., necessary to use the knowledge is considered to be embedded in the knowledge itself.

Procedural knowledge answers the question 'What can you do?' While declarative knowledge is demonstrated using nouns,

Procedural knowledge relies on action words, or verbs.

It is a person's ability to carry out actions to complete a task.

The real difference between declarative and procedural views of knowledge lies in which the control information presides.

Example:

1.

3.

The statements ***1, 2 and 3 are procedural knowledge*** and ***4 is a declarative knowledge.***

Forward & Backward Reasoning

The object of a search procedure is to discover a path through a problem space from an initial configuration to a goal state. There are actually two directions in which such a search could proceed:

Forward Reasoning,

- from the start states
- LHS rule must match with initial state
- Eg: $A \rightarrow B$, $B \rightarrow C \Rightarrow A \rightarrow C$

Backward Reasoning,

- from the goal states
- RHS rules must match with goal state
- Eg: 8-Puzzle Problem

In both the cases, the control strategy is it must cause motion and systematic. The production system model of the search process provides an easy way of viewing forward and backward reasoning as symmetric processes.

Consider the problem of solving a particular instance of the 8-puzzle problem. The rules to be used for solving the puzzle can be written as:

Reasoning Forward from Initial State:

- Begin building a tree of move sequences that might be solved with initial configuration at root of the tree.
- Generate the next level of the tree by finding all the rules whose left sides match the root node and using their right sides to create the new configurations.
- Generate the next level by taking each node generated at the previous level and applying to it all of the rules whose left sides match it.
- Continue until a configuration that matches the goal state is generated.

Reasoning Backward from Goal State:

- Begin building a tree of move sequences that might be solved with goal configuration at root of the tree.
- Generate the next level of the tree by finding all the rules whose right sides match the root node. These are all the rules that, if only we could apply them, would generate the

state we want. Use the left sides of the rules to generate the nodes at this second level of the tree.

- Generate the next level of the tree by taking each node at the previous level and finding all the rules whose right sides match it. Then use the corresponding left sides to generate the new nodes.
- Continue until a node that matches the initial state is generated.
- This method of reasoning backward from the desired final state is often called goal-directed reasoning.

To **reason forward**, the left sides (preconditions) are matched against the current state and the right sides (results) are used to generate new nodes until the goal is reached. To **reason backward**, the right sides are matched against the current node and the left sides are used togenerate new nodes representing new goal states to be achieved.

The following 4 factors influence whether it is better to reason Forward or Backward:

1. Are there more possible start states or goal states? We would like to move from the smaller set of states to the larger (and thus easier to find) set of states.
2. In which direction branching factor (i.e, average number of nodes that can be reached directly from a single node) is greater? We would like to proceed in the direction with lower branching factor.
3. Will the program be used to justify its reasoning process to a user? If so, it is important to proceed in the direction that corresponds more closely with the way the user will think.
4. What kind of event is going to trigger a problem-solving episode? If it is arrival of a new fact, forward reasoning makes sense. If it is a query to which a response is desired, backward reasoning is more natural.

Backward-Chaining Rule Systems

- Backward-chaining rule systems are good for goal-directed problem solving.
- For example, a query system would probably use backward chaining to reason about and answer user questions.
- Unification tries to find a set of bindings for variables to equate a (sub) goal with the head of some rule.
- Medical expert system, diagnostic problems

Forward-Chaining Rule Systems

- Instead of being directed by goals, we sometimes want to be directed by incoming data.
- For example, suppose you sense searing heat near your hand. You are likely to jerk your hand away.
- Rules that match dump their right-hand side assertions into the state and the process repeats.
- Matching is typically more complex for forward-chaining systems than backward ones.
- Synthesis systems – Design/Configuration

Example of Typical Forward Chaining

Rules

1) If hot and smoky then ADD fire
2) If alarm_beeps then ADD smoky
3) If fire then ADD switchon_sprinkles

Facts

1) alarm_beeps (given)
2) hot (given)

....

(3) smoky (from F1 by R2)
(4) fire (from F2, F4 by R1)
(5) switch_on_sprinklers (from F2 by R3)

Example of Typical Backward Chaining

Goal: Should I switch on sprinklers?

Combining Forward and Backward Reasoning

Sometimes certain aspects of a problem are best handled via forward chaining and other aspects by backward chaining. Consider a forward-chaining medical diagnosis program. It might accept twenty or so facts about a patient's condition then forward chain on those concepts to try to deduce the nature and/or cause of the disease.

Now suppose that at some point, the left side of a rule was nearly satisfied – nine out of ten of its preconditions were met. It might be efficient to apply backward reasoning to satisfy the tenth precondition in a directed manner, rather than wait for forward chaining to supply the fact by accident.

Whether it is possible to use the same rules for both forward and backward reasoning also depends on the form of the rules themselves. If both left sides and right sides contain pure assertions, then forward chaining can match assertions on the left side of a rule and add to the state description the assertions on the right side. But if arbitrary procedures are allowed as the right sides of rules then the rules will not be reversible.

Logic Programming

- Logic Programming is a programming language paradigm in which logical assertions are viewed as programs.
- There are several logic programming systems in use today, the most popular of which is PROLOG.
- A PROLOG program is described as a series of logical assertions, each of which is a Horn clause.
- A Horn clause is a clause that has at most one positive literal. Thus p, p q, p → q are all Horn clauses.

Programs written in pure PROLOG are composed only of Horn Clauses.

Syntactic Difference between the logic and the PROLOG representations, including:

- *In logic, variables are explicitly quantified. In PROLOG, quantification is provided implicitly by the way the variables are interpreted.*
    - *The distinction between variables and constants is made in PROLOG by having all variables begin with uppercase letters and all constants begin with lowercase letters.*
- *In logic, there are explicit symbols for and ( ) and or ( ). In PROLOG, there is an explicit symbol for and (,), but there is none for or.*
- *In logic, implications of the form "p implies q" as written as p→q. In PROLOG, the same implication is written "backward" as q: -p.*

Example:

$$\forall x : pet(x) \wedge small(x) \rightarrow apartmentpet(x)$$
$$\forall x : cat(x) \vee dog(x) \rightarrow pet(x)$$
$$\forall x : poodle(x) \rightarrow dog(x) \wedge small(x)$$
$$poodle(ftujfy)$$

A Representation In Logic

```
apartmentpet(X) :- pet(X), small(X).
pet(X) :- cat(X).
pet(X) :- dog(X).
dog(X) :- poodle (X) .
small(X) :- poodle(X).
poodle(fluffy).
```

A Representation in PROLOG

A Declarative and a Procedural Representation

The first two of these differences arise naturally from the fact that PROLOG programs are actually sets of Horn Clauses that have been transformed as follows:

1. If the Horn Clause contains no negative literals (i.e., it contains a single literal which is positive), then leave it as it is.
2. Otherwise, return the Horn clause as an implication, combining all of the negative literals into the antecedent of the implication and leaving the single positive literal (if there is one) as the consequent.

This procedure causes a clause, which originally consisted of a disjunction of literals (all but one of which were negative), to be transformed to single implication whose antecedent is a conjunction of (what are now positive) literals.

$\forall x : \forall y : cat(x) \wedge fish(y) \rightarrow likes\text{-}to\text{-}eat(x, y)$
$\forall x : calico(x) \rightarrow cat(x)$
$\forall x : tuna(x) \rightarrow fish(x)$
$tuna(Charlie)$
$tuna(Herb)$
$calico(Puss)$

(a) Convert these wff's into Horn clauses.
(b) Convert the Horn clauses into a PROLOG program.
(c) Write a PROLOG query corresponding to the question, "What does Puss like to eat?" and show how it will be answered by your program.

(a) Horn clauses:

1. $\neg cat(x) \vee \neg fish(y) \vee likes\text{-}to\text{-}eat(x, y)$
2. $\neg calico(x) \vee cat(x)$
3. $\neg tuna(x) \vee fish(x)$
4. $tuna(Charlie)$
5. $tuna(Herb)$
6. $calico(Puss)$

(b) PROLOG program:

```
likestoeat(X,Y)  :- cat(X),  fish(Y).
cat(X)  :- calico(X).
fish(X)  :- tuna(X).
tuna(charlie).
tuna(herb).
calico(puss).
```

(c) Query:

```
?- likestoeat(puss,X).
```

Answer: `charlie`

Matching

We described the process of using search to solve problems as the application of appropriate rules to individual problem states to generate new states to which the rules can then be applied and so forth until a solution is found.

How we extract from the entire collection of rules those that can be applied at a given point? To do so requires some kind of matching between the current state and the preconditions of the rules. How should this be done? The answer to this question can be critical to the success of a rule based system.

A more complex matching is required when the preconditions of rule specify required properties that are not stated explicitly in the description of the current state. In this case, a separate set of rules must be used to describe how some properties can be inferred from others. An even more complex matching process is required if rules should be applied and if their pre condition approximately match the current situation. This is often the case in situations involving physical descriptions of the world.

Indexing

One way to select applicable rules is to do a simple search though all the rules comparing each one's precondition to the current state and extracting all the one's that match. There are two problems with this simple solution:

i. The large number of rules will be necessary and scanning through all of them at every step would be inefficient.
ii. It's not always obvious whether a rule's preconditions are satisfied by a particular state.

Solution: Instead of searching through rules use the current state as an index into the rules and select the matching one's immediately.

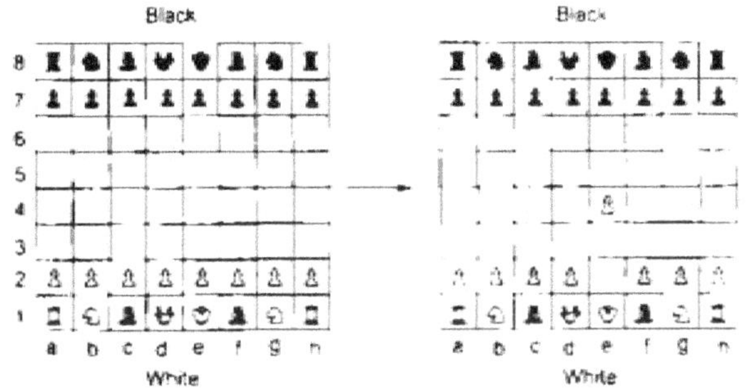

One Legal Chess Move

White pawn at
Square(file e, rank 2)
AND
Square(file e, rank 3)
is empty
AND
Square(file e, rank 4)
is empty

→ move pawn from
Square(file e, rank 2)
to Square(file e, rank 4)

Another Way to Describe Chess Moves

Matching process is easy but at the price of complete lack of generality in the statement of the rules. Despite some limitations of this approach, Indexing in some form is very important in the efficient operation of rule based systems.

Matching with Variables

The problem of selecting applicable rules is made more difficult when preconditions are not stated as exact descriptions of particular situations but rather describe properties that the situations must have. It often turns out that discovering whether there is a match between a particular situation and the preconditions of a given rule must itself involve a significant search process.

Backward-chaining systems usually use depth-first backtracking to select individual rules, but forward-chaining systems generally employ sophisticated conflict resolution strategies to choose among the applicable rules.

While it is possible to apply unification repeatedly over the cross product of preconditions and state description elements, it is more efficient to consider the many-many match problem, in which many rules are matched against many elements in the state description simultaneously. One efficient many-many match algorithm is RETE.

RETE Matching Algorithm

The matching consists of 3 parts

1. Rules & Productions
2. Working Memory
3. Inference Engine

The inference Engine is a cycle of production system which is match, select, execute.

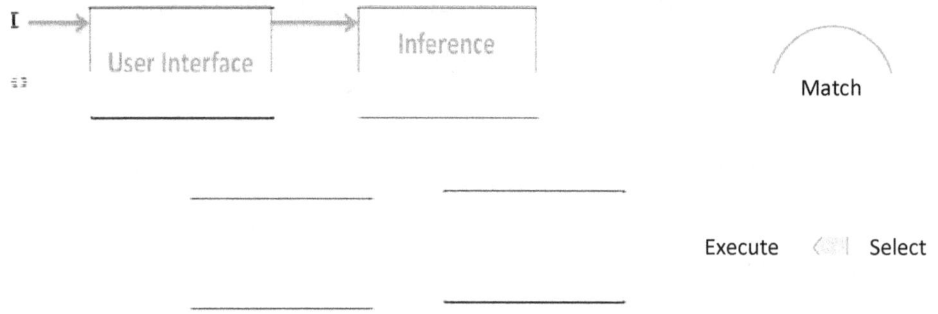

INFERENCE ENGINE

The above cycle is repeated until no rules are put in the conflict set or until stopping condition is reached. In order to verify several conditions, it is a time consuming process. To eliminate the need to perform thousands of matches of cycles on effective matching algorithm is called RETE.

The Algorithm consists of two Steps.

1. Working memory changes need to be examined.
2. Grouping rules which share the same condition & linking them to their common terms.

RETE Algorithm is many-match algorithm (In which many rules are matched against many elements). RETE uses forward chaining systems which generally employee sophisticated conflict resolution strategies to choose among applicable rules. RETE gains efficiency from 3 major sources.

1. RETE maintains a network of rule condition and it uses changes in the state description to determine which new rules might apply. Full matching is only pursued for candidates that could be affected by incoming/outgoing data.
2. Structural Similarity in rules: RETE stores the rules so that they share structures in memory, set of conditions that appear in several rules are matched once for cycle.
3. Persistence of variable binding consistency. While all the individual preconditions of the rule might be met, there may be variable binding conflicts that prevent the rule from firing.

   can be minimized. RETE remembers its previous calculations and is able to merge new binding information efficiently.

Approximate Matching:

Rules should be applied if their preconditions approximately match to the current situation

Eg: Speech understanding program

Rules: A description of a physical waveform to phones

Physical Signal: difference in the way individuals speak, result of background noise.

Conflict Resolution:

When several rules matched at once such a situation is called conflict resolution. There are 3 approaches to the problem of conflict resolution in production system.

1. Preference based on rule match:
    a. Physical order of rules in which they are presented to the system
    b. Priority is given to rules in the order in which they appear

2. Preference based on the objects match:
    a. Considers importance of objects that are matched
    b. Considers the position of the match able objects in terms of Long Term Memory (LTM) & Short Term Memory(STM)

       LTM: Stores a set of rules

       STM (Working Memory): Serves as storage area for the facts deduced by rules in long term memory
3. Preference based on the Action:
    a. One way to do is find all the rules temporarily and examine the results of each. Using a Heuristic Function that can evaluate each of the resulting states compare the merits of the result and then select the preferred one.

Search Control Knowledge:

- It is knowledge about which paths are most likely to lead quickly to a goal state
- Search Control Knowledge requires Meta Knowledge.
- It can take many forms. Knowledge about
    - which states are more preferable to others.
    - which rule to apply in a given situation
    - the Order in which to pursue sub goals
    - useful Sequences of rules to apply.

CONCEPT LEARNING

Concept learning is the task of inferring a Boolean-valued function from training examples of its input and output. We illustrate every step with the classic EnjoySport example.

1. The EnjoySport Learning Task

Target concept: Days on which John enjoys his favourite water sport. Each day is described by six attributes.

Ex	Sky	AirTemp	Humidity	Wind	Water	Forecast	EnjoySport
1	Sunny	Warm	Normal	Strong	Warm	Same	Yes
2	Sunny	Warm	High	Strong	Warm	Same	Yes
3	Rainy	Cold	High	Strong	Warm	Change	No
4	Sunny	Warm	High	Strong	Cool	Change	Yes

2. Hypothesis Representation

Each hypothesis is a vector of six constraints, one per attribute. A constraint may be:

• a specific value (e.g. Sky = Sunny)
• the token ANY meaning any value is acceptable
• the token null meaning no value is acceptable (empty / most-specific hypothesis)

Example hypotheses (written as 6-tuples):

h1 = (Sunny, ANY, ANY, Strong, ANY, ANY) -- Sunny sky and Strong wind

h2 = (ANY, ANY, ANY, ANY, ANY, ANY) -- most general (every day positive)

h3 = (null, null, null, null, null, null) -- most specific (no day positive)

3. The FIND-S Algorithm

FIND-S finds the most specific hypothesis consistent with the positive training examples.

Algorithm FIND-S

1. Initialise h to the most specific hypothesis in H
2. For each positive training instance x
For each attribute constraint a_i in h
If the constraint a_i is satisfied by x, do nothing
Else replace a_i by the next more general constraint that is satisfied by x
3. Output hypothesis h

Trace on the EnjoySport data

Start: h = (null, null, null, null, null, null)

Ex 1 (+) (Sunny, Warm, Normal, Strong, Warm, Same)

h = (Sunny, Warm, Normal, Strong, Warm, Same)

Ex 2 (+) (Sunny, Warm, High, Strong, Warm, Same)

Humidity fails - generalise to ANY

h = (Sunny, Warm, ANY, Strong, Warm, Same)

Ex 3 is negative - ignored by FIND-S

Ex 4 (+) (Sunny, Warm, High, Strong, Cool, Change)

Water and Forecast fail - generalise both to ANY

h = (Sunny, Warm, ANY, Strong, ANY, ANY)

FIND-S is guaranteed to output the most specific hypothesis consistent with the positive examples (and with all examples if the target is in H and the data are noise-free).

Python - FIND-S

```
def find_s(examples):
    """examples: list of (attr_tuple, label) where label is True/False"""
    h = None
    for x, label in examples:
        if not label:
            continue
        if h is None:
            h = list(x)
        else:
            for i in range(len(h)):
                if h[i] != x[i]:
                    h[i] = 'ANY'
    return tuple(h) if h else None

data = [
    (('Sunny','Warm','Normal','Strong','Warm','Same'), True),
    (('Sunny','Warm','High','Strong','Warm','Same'), True),
    (('Rainy','Cold','High','Strong','Warm','Change'), False),
    (('Sunny','Warm','High','Strong','Cool','Change'), True),
]
print("FIND-S result:", find_s(data))
# -> ('Sunny', 'Warm', 'ANY', 'Strong', 'ANY', 'ANY')
```

4. Version Spaces and Candidate-Elimination

The version space VS(H,D) is the set of all hypotheses in H consistent with training data D. It is represented by two boundary sets:

- S - the set of most specific members of the version space
- G - the set of most general members of the version space

Every hypothesis between (more general than) S and (more specific than) G also belongs to the version space.

Candidate-Elimination Algorithm

1. Initialise G = { (ANY, ANY, ANY, ANY, ANY, ANY) } (maximally general)
2. Initialise S = { (null, null, null, null, null, null) } (maximally specific)
3. For each training example d:

If d is positive:
- Remove from G any hypothesis inconsistent with d
- For each s in S inconsistent with d: remove s; add all minimal generalisations of s that are consistent with d and still more specific than some member of G; prune S of any hypothesis more general than another in S

If d is negative:
- Remove from S any hypothesis inconsistent with d
- For each g in G inconsistent with d: remove g; add all minimal specialisations of g that are consistent with d and still more general than some member of S; prune G of any hypothesis more specific than another in G

4. Output the version space bounded by S and G

Trace (EnjoySport)

After Ex1 (+): S = {(Sunny, Warm, Normal, Strong, Warm, Same)}

G = {(ANY, ANY, ANY, ANY, ANY, ANY)}

After Ex2 (+): S = {(Sunny, Warm, ANY, Strong, Warm, Same)}

G unchanged

After Ex3 (-): S unchanged

G = {(Sunny,ANY,ANY,ANY,ANY,ANY), (ANY,Warm,ANY,ANY,ANY,ANY), (ANY,ANY,ANY,ANY,ANY,Same)}

After Ex4 (+): S = {(Sunny, Warm, ANY, Strong, ANY, ANY)}

G = {(Sunny,ANY,ANY,ANY,ANY,ANY), (ANY,Warm,ANY,ANY,ANY,ANY)}

The final version space contains every hypothesis more general than S and more specific than G. Any of them may classify a new instance; when they disagree the learner can abstain or take a majority vote.

Python - version-space boundary check

```
def more_general(h1, h2):
    """True if h1 is more general than or equal to h2"""
    for a, b in zip(h1, h2):
        if a != 'ANY' and a != b:
```

```
            return False
    return True

def consistent(h, x, label):
    match = all(a == 'ANY' or a == v for a, v in zip(h, x))
    return match == label

# Final boundaries after the four EnjoySport examples:
S = {('Sunny','Warm','ANY','Strong','ANY','ANY')}
G = {('Sunny','ANY','ANY','ANY','ANY','ANY'), ('ANY','Warm','ANY','ANY','ANY','ANY')}
print("S boundary:", S)
print("G boundary:", G)
```

End of rewritten Concept Learning / FIND-S / Candidate-Elimination section.

MODULE – 2

PART 1 - DECISION TREE LEARNING

Decision tree learning is a method for approximating discrete-valued target functions, in which the learned function is represented by a decision tree.

2.1. Decision Tree Representation

- Decision trees classify instances by sorting them down the tree from the root to some leaf node, which provides the classification of the instance.
- Each node in the tree specifies a test of some attribute of the instance, and each branch descending from that node corresponds to one of the possible values for this attribute.
- An instance is classified by starting at the root node of the tree, testing the attribute specified by this node, then moving down the tree branch corresponding to the value of the attribute in the given example. This process is then repeated for the subtree rooted at the new node.

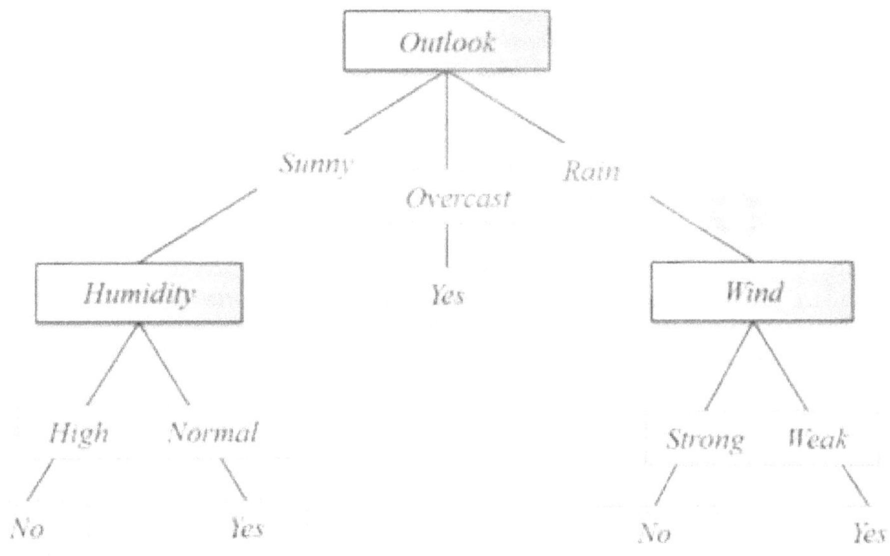

Figure: Decision tree for the concept ***PlayTennis***. An example is classified by sorting it through the tree to the appropriate leaf node, then returning the classification associated with the leaf.

- Decision trees represent a disjunction of conjunctions of constraints on the attribute values of instances.
- Each path from the tree root to a leaf corresponds to a conjunction of attribute tests, and the tree itself to a disjunction of these conjunctions
- For example, the decision tree shown in above figure corresponds to the expression

(Outlook = Sunny   Humidity = Normal)
(Outlook = Overcast)
(Outlook = Rain   Wind = Weak)

2.2. Appropriate Problems for Decision Tree Learning

Decision tree learning is generally best suited to problems with the following characteristics:

i. ***Instances are represented by attribute-value pairs*** – Instances are described by a fixed set of attributes and their values
ii. ***The target function has discrete output values*** – The decision tree assigns a Boolean classification (e.g., yes or no) to each example. Decision tree methods easily extend to learning functions with more than two possible output values.
iii. ***Disjunctive descriptions may be required***
iv. ***The training data may contain errors*** – Decision tree learning methods are robust to errors, both errors in classifications of the training examples and errors in the attribute values that describe these examples.
v. ***The training data may contain missing attribute values*** – Decision tree methods can be used even when some training examples have unknown values.

2.3. The Basic Decision Tree Learning Algorithm

The basic algorithm is ID3 which learns decision trees by constructing them top-down.

ID3(Examples, Target_attribute, Attributes)

Examples are the training examples.

Target_attribute is the attribute whose value is to be predicted by the tree.

Attributes is a list of other attributes that may be tested by the learned decision tree.

Returns a decision tree that correctly classifies the given Examples.

- Create a Root node for the tree
- If all Examples are positive, Return the single-node tree Root, with label = +
- If all Examples are negative, Return the single-node tree Root, with label = -
- If Attributes is empty, Return the single-node tree Root, with label = most common value of Target_attribute in Examples
- Otherwise Begin
    - A ← the attribute from Attributes that best* classifies Examples
    - The decision attribute for Root ← A
    - For each possible value, *vi*, of A,
        - Add a new tree branch below *Root*, corresponding to the test A = *vi*
        - Let *Examples vi*, be the subset of Examples that have value *vi* for *A*
        - If *Examples vi* , is empty
            - Then below this new branch add a leaf node with label = most common value of Target_attribute in Examples
            - Else below this new branch add the subtree
                - ID3(*Examples vi*, Target_attribute, Attributes – {A}))
- End
- Return Root

---

* The best attribute is the one with highest information gain

Table: Summary of the ID3 algorithm specialized to learning Boolean-valued functions. ID3 is a greedy algorithm that grows the tree top-down, at each node selecting the attribute that best classifies the local training examples. This process continues until the tree perfectly classifies the training examples, or until all attributes have been used.

Which attribute is a best classifier?

- The central choice in the ID3 algorithm is selecting which attribute to test at each node in the tree.
- A statistical property called ***information gain*** that measures how well a given attribute separates the training examples according to their target classification.
- ID3 uses ***information gain*** measure to select among the candidate attributes at each step while growing the tree.

2.4. Entropy Measures Homogeneity of Examples

To define information gain, we begin by defining a measure called entropy. *Entropy measures the impurity of a collection of examples.*

Given a collection S, containing positive and negative examples of some target concept, the entropy of S relative to this Boolean classification is

$$\text{Entropy}(S) \equiv -p_{\oplus} \log_2 p_{\oplus} - p_{\ominus} \log_2 p_{\ominus}$$

Where,

$p+ \rightarrow$ proportion of positive examples in S

$p- \rightarrow$ proportion of negative examples in S.

Example:

Suppose S is a collection of 14 examples of some boolean concept, including 9 positive and 5 negative examples. Then the entropy of S relative to this boolean classification is

$$Entropy([9+,5-]) = -(9/14)\log_2(9/14) - (5/14)\log_2(5/14) = 0.940$$

- The entropy is 0 if all members of S belong to the same class
- The entropy is 1 when the collection contains an equal number of positive and negative examples
- If the collection contains unequal numbers of positive and negative examples, the entropy is between 0 and 1.

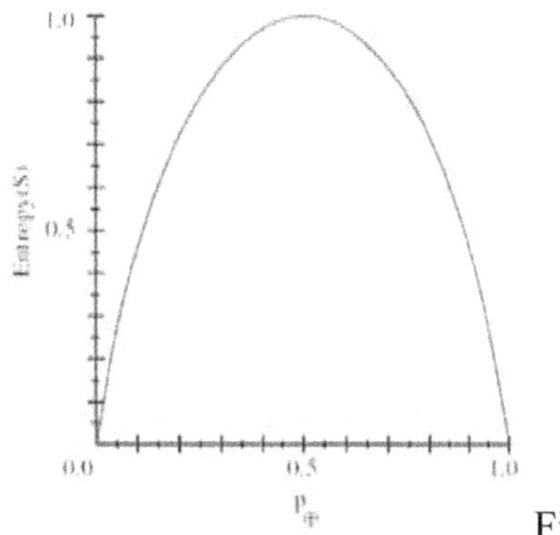

Figure: The Entropy relative to a Boolean classification, as the proportion of positive examples varies from 0 to 1.

2.5. Information Gain Measures the Expected Reduction in Entropy

Information Gain, is the expected reduction in entropy caused by partitioning the examples according to this attribute.

The information gain, Gain(S, A) of an attribute A, relative to a collection of examples S, is defined as

$$Gain(S, A) = Entropy(S) - \sum_{v \in Values(A)} \frac{|S_v|}{|S|} Entropy(S_v)$$

Example,

Let,

$Values(Wind) = \{Weak, Strong\}$

$S = [9+, 5-]$

$S_{Weak} = [6+, 2-]$

$S_{Strong} = [3+, 3-]$

Information gain of attribute *Wind*:

$Gain(S, Wind) = Entropy(S) - 8/14\ Entropy(S_{Weak}) - 6/14\ Entropy(S_{Strong})$

$= 0.94 - (8/14)*0.811 - (6/14)*1.00$

$= 0.048$

An Illustrative Example

- To illustrate the operation of ID3, consider the learning task represented by the training examples of below table.
- Here the target attribute ***PlayTennis***, which can have values ***yes*** or ***no*** for different days.
- Consider the first step through the algorithm, in which the topmost node of the decision tree is created.

Example	Outlook	Temperature	Humidity	Wind	PlayTennis
D1	sunny	hot	high	weak	No
D2	sunny	hot	high	strong	No
D3	overcast	hot	high	weak	Yes
D4	rain	mild	high	weak	Yes
D5	rain	cool	normal	weak	Yes
D6	rain	cool	normal	strong	No

D7	overcast	cool	normal	strong	Yes
D8	sunny	mild	high	weak	No
D9	sunny	cool	normal	weak	Yes
D10	rain	mild	normal	weak	Yes
D11	sunny	mild	normal	strong	Yes
D12	overcast	mild	high	strong	Yes
D13	overcast	hot	normal	weak	Yes
D14	rain	mild	high	strong	No

ID3 determines the information gain for each candidate attribute (i.e., Outlook, Temperature, Humidity, and Wind), then selects the one with highest information gain.

Which attribute is a best classifier?

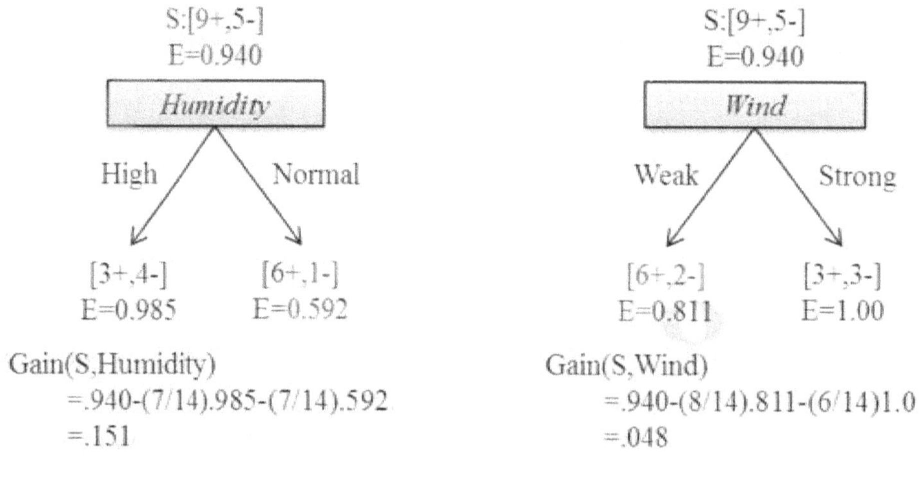

The information gain values for all four attributes are

Gain(S, Outlook) = 0.247

Gain(S,Temperature) = 0.028

Gain(S, Humidity) = 0.151

Gain(S,Wind) = 0.048

According to the information gain measure, the ***Outlook*** attribute provides the best prediction of the target attribute, ***PlayTennis***, over the training examples. Therefore, ***Outlook*** is selected as the decision attribute for the root node, and branches are createdbelow the root for each of its possible values i.e., Sunny, Overcast, and Rain.

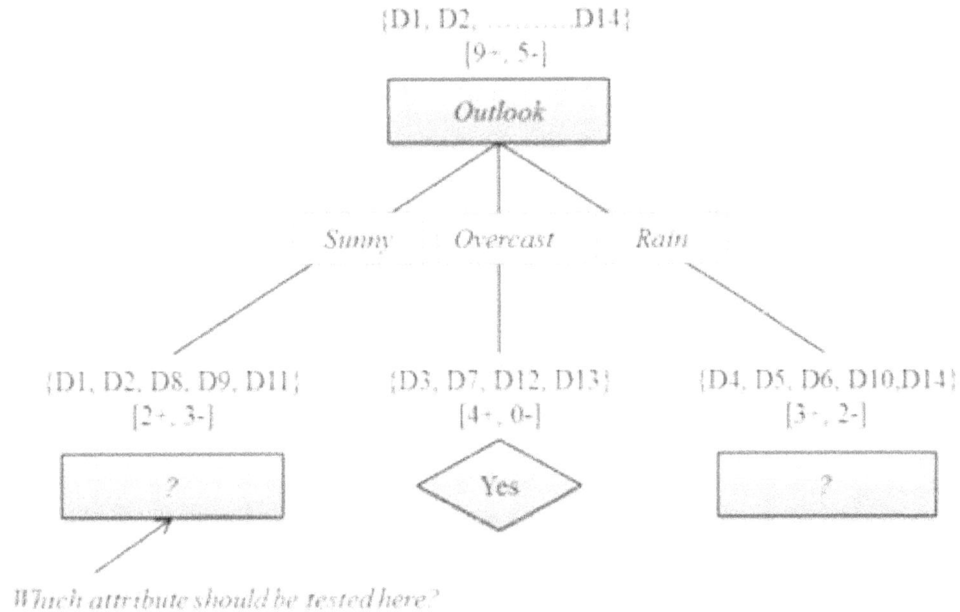

$S_{sunny} = \{D1, D2, D8, D9, D11\}$

$Gain(S_{sunny}, Humidity) = .970 - (3/5)0.0 - (2/5)0.0 = .970$

$Gain(S_{sunny}, Temperature) = .970 - (2/5)0.0 - (2/5)1.0 - (1/5)0.0 = .570$

$Gain(S_{sunny}, Wind) = .970 - (2/5)1.0 - (3/5).918 = .019$

$S_{rain} = \{D4, D5, D6, D10, D14\}$

$Gain(S_{rain}, Humidity) = .970 - (2/5)1.0 - (3/5).917 = .019$

$Gain(S_{rain}, Temperature) = .970 - (0/5)0.0 - (3/5).918 - (2/5)1.0 = .019$

$Gain(S_{rain}, Wind) = .970 - (3/5)0.0 - (2/5)0.0 = .970$

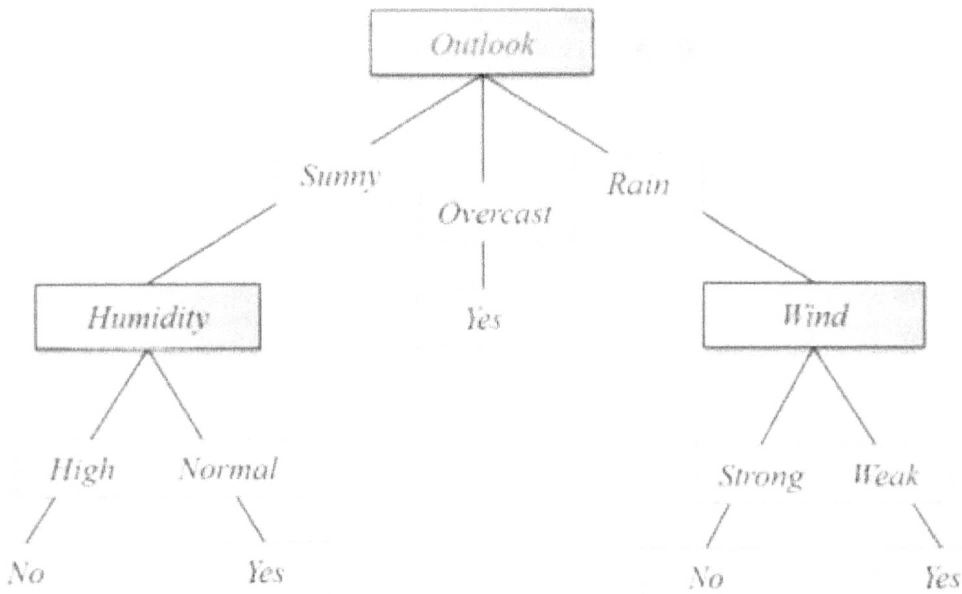

2.6. Hypothesis Space Search in Decision Tree Learning

- ID3 can be characterized as searching a space of hypotheses for one that fits the training examples.
- The hypothesis space searched by ID3 is the set of possible decision trees.
- ID3 performs a simple-to complex, hill-climbing search through this hypothesis space, beginning with the empty tree, then considering progressively more elaborate hypotheses in search of a decision tree that correctly classifies the training data.

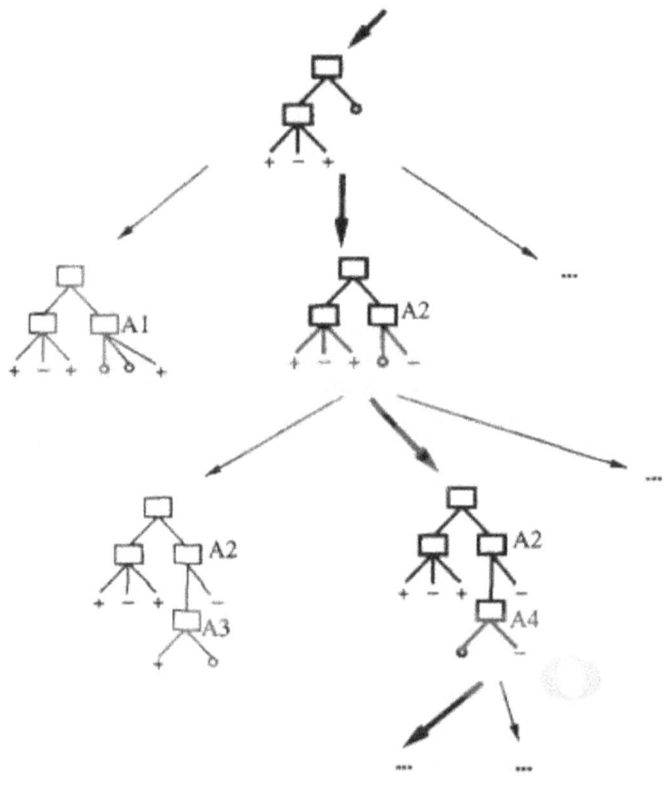

Figure: Hypothesis space search by ID3. ID3 searches through the space of possible decision trees from simplest to increasingly complex, guided by the information gain heuristic.

By viewing ID3 in terms of its search space and search strategy, there are some insight into its capabilities and limitations

1. *ID3's hypothesis space of all decision trees is a complete space of finite discrete-valued functions, relative to the available attributes. Because every finite discrete-valued function can be represented by some decision tree*

   ID3 avoids one of the major risks of methods that search incomplete hypothesis spaces: that the hypothesis space might not contain the target function.

2. *ID3 maintains only a single current hypothesis as it searches through the space of decision trees.*

For example, with the earlier version space candidate elimination method, which maintains the set of all hypotheses consistent with the available training examples.

By determining only a single hypothesis, ID3 loses the capabilities that follow from explicitly representing all consistent hypotheses.

For example, it does not have the ability to determine how many alternative decision trees are consistent with the available training data, or to pose new instance queries that optimally resolve among these competing hypotheses

3. *ID3 in its pure form performs no backtracking in its search. Once it selects an attribute to test at a particular level in the tree, it never backtracks to reconsider this choice.*

In the case of ID3, a locally optimal solution corresponds to the decision tree it selects along the single search path it explores. However, this locally optimal solution may be less desirable than trees that would have been encountered along a different branch of the search.

4. *ID3 uses all training examples at each step in the search to make statistically based decisions regarding how to refine its current hypothesis.*

One advantage of using statistical properties of all the examples is that the resulting search is much less sensitive to errors in individual training examples.

ID3 can be easily extended to handle noisy training data by modifying its termination criterion to accept hypotheses that imperfectly fit the training data.

2.7. Inductive Bias in Decision Tree Learning

Inductive bias is the set of assumptions that, together with the training data, deductively justify the classifications assigned by the learner to future instances.

Given a collection of training examples, there are typically many decision trees consistent with these examples. Which of these decision trees does ID3 choose?

ID3 search strategy

- Selects in favor of shorter trees over longer ones
- Selects trees that place the attributes with highest information gain closest to the root.

Approximate inductive bias of ID3: Shorter trees are preferred over larger trees

- Consider an algorithm that begins with the empty tree and searches breadth first through progressively more complex trees.
- First considering all trees of depth 1, then all trees of depth 2, etc.
- Once it finds a decision tree consistent with the training data, it returns the smallest consistent tree at that search depth (e.g., the tree with the fewest nodes).
- Let us call this breadth-first search algorithm BFS-ID3.
- BFS-ID3 finds a shortest decision tree and thus exhibits the bias "shorter trees are preferred over longer trees.

  A closer approximation to the inductive bias of ID3: Shorter trees are preferred over longer trees. Trees that place high information gain attributes close to the root are preferred over those that do not.

- ID3 can be viewed as an efficient approximation to BFS-ID3, using a greedy heuristic search to attempt to find the shortest tree without conducting the entire breadth-first search through the hypothesis space.
- Because ID3 uses the information gain heuristic and a hill climbing strategy, it exhibits a more complex bias than BFS-ID3.
- In particular, it does not always find the shortest consistent tree, and it is biased to favor trees that place attributes with high information gain closest to the root.

Restriction Biases and Preference Biases

Difference between the types of inductive bias exhibited by ID3 and by the CANDIDATE-ELIMINATION Algorithm.

ID3:

- ID3 searches a complete hypothesis space
- It searches incompletely through this space, from simple to complex hypotheses, until its termination condition is met
- Its inductive bias is solely a consequence of the ordering of hypotheses by its search strategy. Its hypothesis space introduces no additional bias.

CANDIDATE-ELIMINATION Algorithm:

- The version space CANDIDATE-ELIMINATION Algorithm searches an incomplete hypothesis space
- It searches this space completely, finding every hypothesis consistent with the training data.
- Its inductive bias is solely a consequence of the expressive power of its hypothesis representation. Its search strategy introduces no additional bias.

Preference bias – The inductive bias of ID3 is a preference for certain hypotheses over others (e.g., preference for shorter hypotheses over larger hypotheses), with no hard restriction on the hypotheses that can be eventually enumerated. This form of bias is called a preference bias or a search bias.

Restriction bias – The bias of the CANDIDATE ELIMINATION algorithm is in the form of a categorical restriction on the set of hypotheses considered. This form of bias is typically called a restriction bias or a language bias.

Which type of inductive bias is preferred in order to generalize beyond the training data, a preference bias or restriction bias?

- A preference bias is more desirable than a restriction bias, because it allows the learner to work within a complete hypothesis space that is assured to contain the unknown target function.
- In contrast, a restriction bias that strictly limits the set of potential hypotheses is generally less desirable, because it introduces the possibility of excluding the unknown target function altogether.

Why Prefer Short Hypotheses?

Occam's razor

- Occam's razor: is the problem-solving principle that the simplest solution tends to be the right one. When presented with competing hypotheses to solve a problem, one should select the solution with the fewest assumptions.
- Occam's razor: "Prefer the simplest hypothesis that fits the data".

Argument in favour of Occam's razor:

- Fewer short hypotheses than long ones:
    - o Short hypotheses fits the training data which are less likely to be coincident
    - o Longer hypotheses fits the training data might be coincident.
- Many complex hypotheses that fit the current training data but fail to generalize correctly to subsequent data.

Argument opposed:

- There are few small trees, and our priori chance of finding one consistent with an arbitrary set of data is therefore small. The difficulty here is that there are very many small sets of hypotheses that one can define but understood by fewer learner.
- The size of a hypothesis is determined by the representation used internally by the learner. Occam's razor will produce two different hypotheses from the same training examples when it is applied by two learners, both justifying their contradictory conclusions by Occam's razor. On this basis we might be tempted to reject Occam's razor altogether.

2.8. Issues in Decision Tree Learning

Issues in learning decision trees include

1. Avoiding Overfitting the Data
    - o Reduced error pruning
    - o Rule post-pruning
2. Incorporating Continuous-Valued Attributes
3. Alternative Measures for Selecting Attributes
4. Handling Training Examples with Missing Attribute Values
5. Handling Attributes with Differing Costs

1. Avoiding Overfitting the Data

o The ID3 algorithm grows each branch of the tree just deeply enough to perfectly classify the training examples but it can lead to difficulties when there is noise in the data, or when the number of training examples is too small to produce a representative sample of the true target function. This algorithm can produce trees that overfit the training examples.

o***Definition - Overfit:*** Given a hypothesis space H, a hypothesis h ∈ H is said to overfit the training data if there exists some alternative hypothesis h' ∈ H, such that h has smaller error than h' over the training examples, but h' has a smaller error than h over the entire distribution of instances.

The below figure illustrates the impact of overfitting in a typical application of decision tree learning.

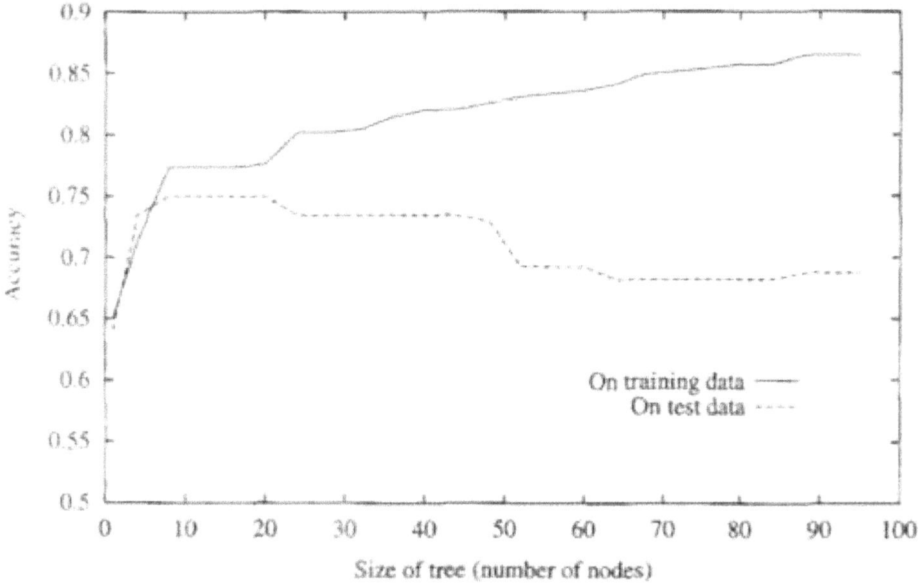

- *The horizontal axis* of this plot indicates the total number of nodes in the decision tree, as the tree is being constructed. The vertical axis indicates the accuracy of predictions made by the tree.
- *The solid line* shows the accuracy of the decision tree over the training examples. The broken line shows accuracy measured over an independent set of test example
- The accuracy of the tree over the training examples increases monotonically as the tree is grown. The accuracy measured over the independent test examples first increases, then decreases.

How can it be possible for tree h to fit the training examples better than h', but for it to perform more poorly over subsequent examples?

i. Overfitting can occur when the training examples contain random errors or noise

ii. When small numbers of examples are associated with leaf nodes. Noisy Training Example

- Example 15: <Sunny, Hot, Normal, Strong, ->
- Example is noisy because the correct label is +
- Previously constructed tree misclassifies it.

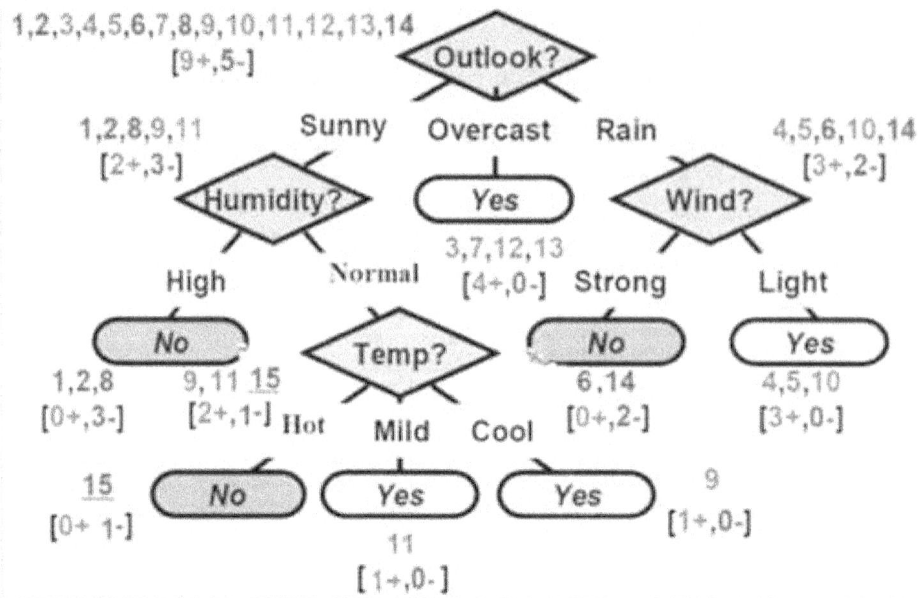

Approaches to avoiding overfitting in decision tree learning

- Pre-pruning (avoidance): Stop growing the tree earlier, before it reaches the point where it perfectly classifies the training data
- Post-pruning (recovery): Allow the tree to overfit the data, and then post-prune the tree Criterion used to determine the correct final tree size

  - Use a separate set of examples, distinct from the training examples, to evaluate the utility of post-pruning nodes from the tree
  - Use all the available data for training, but apply a statistical test to estimate whether expanding (or pruning) a particular node is likely to produce an improvement beyond the training set
  - Use measure of the complexity for encoding the training examples and the decision tree, halting growth of the tree when this encoding size is minimized. This approach is called the Minimum Description Length

MDL – Minimize : size(tree) + size (misclassifications(tree))

Reduced Error Pruning

- Reduced-error pruning, is to consider each of the decision nodes in the tree to be candidates for pruning
- ***Pruning*** a decision node consists of removing the subtree rooted at that node, making it a leaf node, and assigning it the most common classification of the training examples affiliated with that node

- Nodes are removed only if the resulting pruned tree performs no worse than-the original over the validation set.
- Reduced error pruning has the effect that any leaf node added due to coincidental regularities in the training set is likely to be pruned because these same coincidences are unlikely to occur in the validation set

The impact of reduced-error pruning on the accuracy of the decision tree is illustrated in below figure

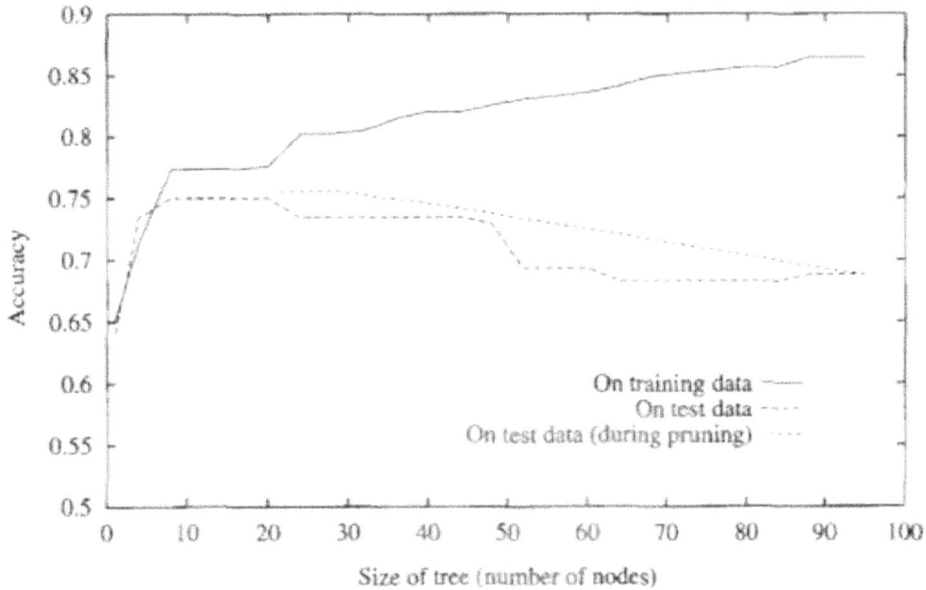

- The additional line in figure shows accuracy over the test examples as the tree is pruned. When pruning begins, the tree is at its maximum size and lowest accuracy over the test set. As pruning proceeds, the number of nodes is reduced and accuracy over the test set increases.
- The available data has been split into three subsets: the training examples, the validation examples used for pruning the tree, and a set of test examples used to provide an unbiased estimate of accuracy over future unseen examples. The plot shows accuracy over the training and test sets.

Pros and Cons

Pro: Produces smallest version of most accurate *T* (subtree of *T*)

Con: Uses less data to construct *T*

Can afford to hold out $D_{validation}$?. If not (data is too limited), may make error worse (insufficient D_{train})

Rule Post-Pruning

Rule post-pruning is successful method for finding high accuracy hypotheses

Rule post-pruning involves the following steps:

- Infer the decision tree from the training set, growing the tree until the training data is fit as well as possible and allowing overfitting to occur.
- Convert the learned tree into an equivalent set of rules by creating one rule for each path from the root node to a leaf node.
- Prune (generalize) each rule by removing any preconditions that result in improving its estimated accuracy.
  - Sort the pruned rules by their estimated accuracy, and consider them in this sequence when classifying subsequent instances.

Converting a Decision Tree into Rules

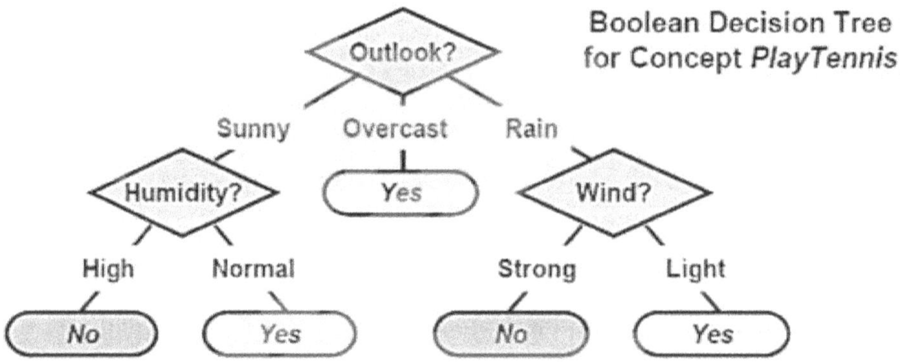

Example

- IF (*Outlook* = *Sunny*) ∧ (*Humidity* = *High*) THEN *PlayTennis* = *No*
- IF (*Outlook* = *Sunny*) ∧ (*Humidity* = *Normal*) THEN *PlayTennis* = *Yes*
- ...

For example, consider the decision tree. The leftmost path of the tree in below figure is translated into the rule.

IF (Outlook = Sunny) ^ (Humidity = High)

THEN PlayTennis = No

Given the above rule, rule post-pruning would consider removing the preconditions (Outlook = Sunny) and (Humidity = High)

- It would select whichever of these pruning steps produced the greatest improvement in estimated rule accuracy, then consider pruning the second precondition as a further pruning step.
- No pruning step is performed if it reduces the estimated rule accuracy.

There are three main advantages by converting the decision tree to rules before pruning

- Converting to rules allows distinguishing among the different contexts in which a decision node is used. Because each distinct path through the decision tree node produces a distinct rule, the pruning decision regarding that attribute test can be made differently for each path.
- Converting to rules removes the distinction between attribute tests that occur near the root of the tree and those that occur near the leaves. Thus, it avoid messy bookkeeping issues such as how to reorganize the tree if the root node is pruned while retaining part of the subtree below this test.
- Converting to rules improves readability. Rules are often easier for to understand.

2. *Incorporating Continuous-Valued Attributes*

Continuous-valued decision attributes can be incorporated into the learned tree. *There are two methods for Handling Continuous Attributes*

i. Define new discrete valued attributes that partition the continuous attribute value into a discrete set of intervals.

E.g., {high ≡ Temp > 35° C, med ≡ 10° C < Temp ≤ 35° C, low ≡ Temp ≤ 10° C}

ii. Using thresholds for splitting nodes

e.g., A ≤ a produces subsets A ≤ a and A > a

What threshold-based Boolean attribute should be defined based on Temperature?

Temperature:	40	48	60	72	80	90
PlayTennis:	No	No	Yes	Yes	Yes	No

- Pick a threshold, c, that produces the greatest information gain
- In the current example, there are two candidate thresholds, corresponding to the values of Temperature at which the value of PlayTennis changes: (48 + 60)/2, and (80 + 90)/2.
- The information gain can then be computed for each of the candidate attributes, Temperature >54, and Temperature >85 and the best can be selected (Temperature >54)

3. Alternative Measures for Selecting Attributes

- The problem is if attributes with many values, Gain will select it ?

- Example: consider the attribute Date, which has a very large number of possible values. (e.g., March 4, 1979).
- If this attribute is added to the PlayTennis data, it would have the highest information gain of any of the attributes. This is because Date alone perfectly predicts the target attribute over the training data. Thus, it would be selected as the decision attribute for the root node of the tree and lead to a tree of depth one, which perfectly classifies the training data.
- This decision tree with root node Date is not a useful predictor because it perfectly separates the training data, but poorly predict on subsequent examples.

One Approach: Use GainRatio instead of Gain

The gain ratio measure penalizes attributes by incorporating a split information, that is sensitive to how broadly and uniformly the attribute splits the data.

$$Gain(S, A) \qquad \frac{Gain(S, A)}{SplitInformation(S, A)}$$

$$SplitInformation(S, A) \quad - \quad {}_{i=1}^{c} \frac{|S_i|}{|S|} \log_2 \frac{|S_i|}{|S|}$$

Where, S_i is a subset of S, for which the attribute A has the value v_i.

4. Handling Training Examples with Missing Attribute Values

The data which is available may contain missing values for some attributes Example: Medical diagnosis.

- <Fever = true, Blood-Pressure = normal, …, Blood-Test = ?, …>
- Sometimes values truly unknown, sometimes low priority (or cost too high)

Strategies for dealing with the missing attribute value

- If node n test A, assign most common value of A among other training examples sorted to node n
- Assign most common value of A among other training examples with same target value
- Assign a probability pi to each of the possible values vi of A rather than simply assigning the most common value to A(x)

5. Handling Attributes with Differing Costs

- In some learning tasks the instance attributes may have associated costs.
- For example: In learning to classify medical diseases, the patients described in terms of attributes such as Temperature, BiopsyResult, Pulse, BloodTestResults, etc.
- These attributes vary significantly in their costs, both in terms of monetary cost and cost to patient comfort
- Decision trees use low-cost attributes where possible, depends only on high-cost attributes only when needed to produce reliable classifications

How to Learn A Consistent Tree with Low Expected Cost?

One approach is replace Gain by Cost-Normalized-Gain

Examples of normalization functions

- Tan and Schimmer

$$\frac{Gain^2(S, A)}{Cost(A)}$$

- Nunez

$$\frac{2^{Gain(S,A)} - 1}{(Cost(A) + 1)^w}$$

Where, w [0,1] determines importance of cost.

PART 2 – ARTIFICIAL NEURAL NETWORKS

INTRODUCTION

Artificial neural networks (ANNs) provide a general, practical method for learning real-valued, discrete-valued, and vector-valued target functions.

Biological Motivation

- The study of artificial neural networks (ANNs) has been inspired by the observation that biological learning systems are built of very complex webs of interconnected

Neurons

- Human information processing system consists of brain ***neuron***: basic building block cell that communicates information to and from various parts of body

Facts of Human Neurobiology

- Number of neurons ~ 10^{11}
- Connection per neuron ~ 10^{4-5}
- Neuron switching time ~ 0.001 second or 10^{-3}
- Scene recognition time ~ 0.1 second
- **100 inference steps doesn't seem like enough**
- Highly parallel computation based on distributed representation

Properties of Neural Networks

- Many neuron-like threshold switching units
- Many weighted interconnections among units
- Highly parallel, distributed process
- Emphasis on tuning weights automatically
- Input is a high-dimensional discrete or real-valued (e.g, sensor input)

3.2. NEURAL NETWORK REPRESENTATIONS

- A prototypical example of ANN learning is provided by Pomerleau's system ALVINN, which uses a learned ANN to steer an autonomous vehicle driving at normal speeds on public highways.

- The input to the neural network is a 30x32 grid of pixel intensities obtained from a forward-pointed camera mounted on the vehicle.The network output is the direction in which the vehicle is steered

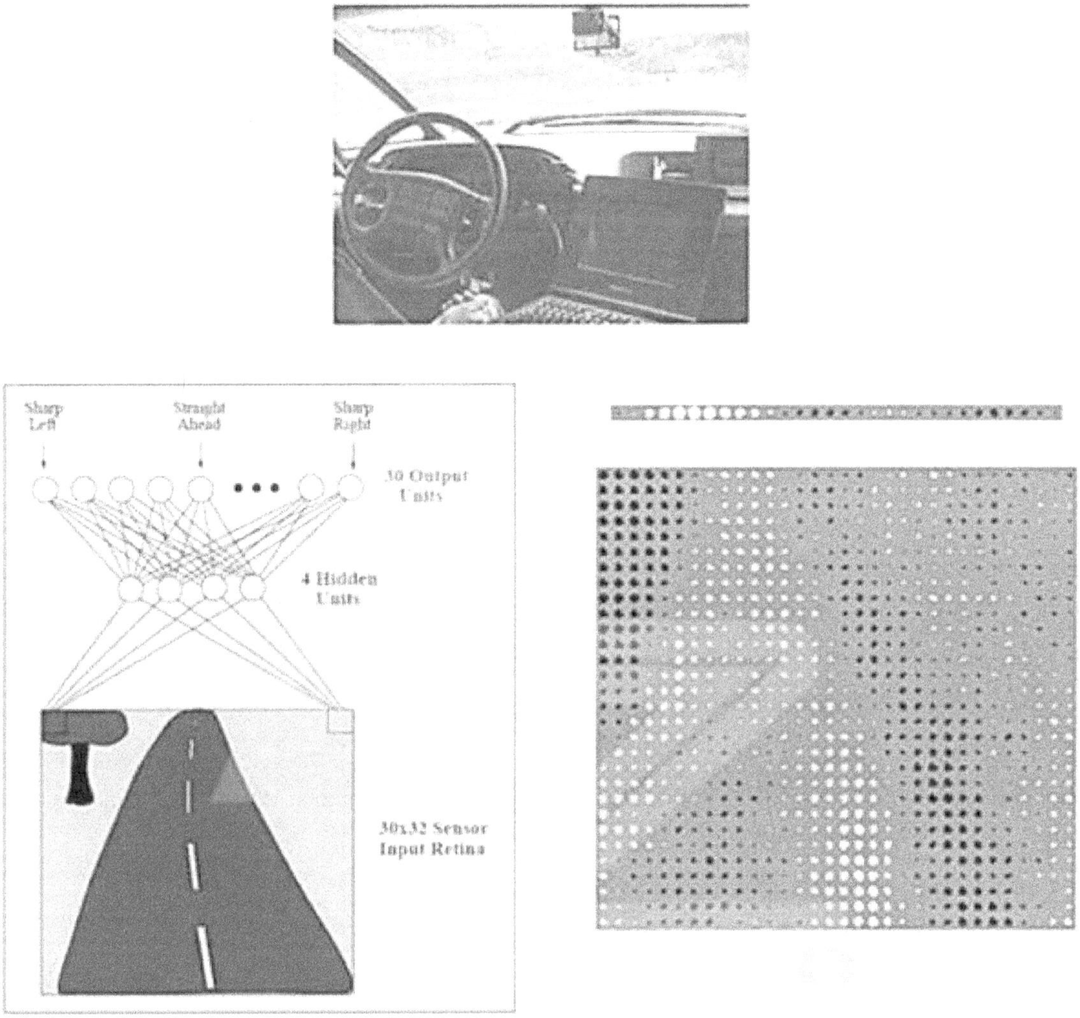

Figure 1: Neural network learning to steer an autonomous vehicle

2. Figure 1 illustrates the neural network representation.
3. The network is shown on the left side of the figure, with the input camera image depicted below it.
4. Each node (i.e., circle) in the network diagram corresponds to the output of a single network unit, and the lines entering the node from below are its inputs.
5. There are four units that receive inputs directly from all of the 30 x 32 pixels in the image. These are called "hidden" units because their output is available only within the network and is not available as part of the global network output. Each

3.4 PERCEPTRON

A perceptron is the simplest neural-network unit. It computes a linear combination of its real-valued inputs and then applies a threshold (or soft) activation.

Perceptron Unit

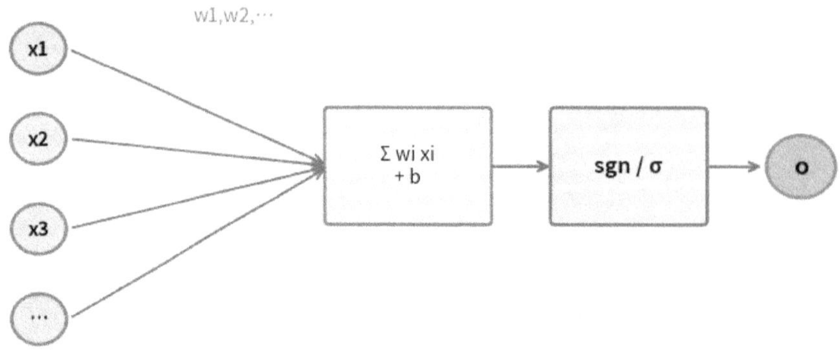

Decision rule (hard threshold)

$$o(x) = \text{sgn}(w \cdot x + b) = +1 \text{ if } \Sigma_i w_i x_i + b > 0, \text{ otherwise } -1.$$

Geometrically the weight vector defines a hyperplane that separates the two classes. The classic perceptron learning rule is guaranteed to find a separating hyperplane whenever the data are linearly separable.

Perceptron training rule

Start with arbitrary weights. For each misclassified example (x, t) apply the update

$$w_i \leftarrow w_i + \eta (t - o) x_i$$

where $\eta > 0$ is the learning rate, $t \in \{+1,-1\}$ is the target and o is the current output. When the example is already correct, (t–o)=0 and the weights are left unchanged.

Python – Perceptron from scratch

```
import numpy as np

class Perceptron:
    def __init__(self, n_features, lr=0.1, epochs=50):
        self.w = np.zeros(n_features)
        self.b = 0.0
        self.lr = lr
        self.epochs = epochs
    def predict(self, X):
        return np.where(X @ self.w + self.b >= 0, 1, 0)
    def fit(self, X, y):
        for _ in range(self.epochs):
            for xi, yi in zip(X, y):
                err = yi - self.predict(xi.reshape(1,-1))[0]
                self.w += self.lr * err * xi
                self.b += self.lr * err
        return self

X = np.array([[0,0],[0,1],[1,0],[1,1]], float)
y = np.array([0,0,0,1])             # AND
clf = Perceptron(2).fit(X, y)
print("Weights:", clf.w, "Bias:", clf.b)
print("Predictions:", clf.predict(X))
```

Gradient Descent and the Delta Rule

When the hard threshold is replaced by a differentiable activation (sigmoid / linear) we can minimise a continuous error function by gradient descent. Define the squared error over the training set:

$$E(w) = \tfrac{1}{2} \Sigma_{d \in D} (t_d - o_d)^2$$

For a linear unit o = w · x the gradient has the closed form

$$\partial E/\partial w_i = -\Sigma_d (t_d - o_d)\, x_{i,d}$$

yielding the **delta (LMS) rule**:

$$\Delta w_i = \eta\, \Sigma_d (t_d - o_d)\, x_{i,d}$$

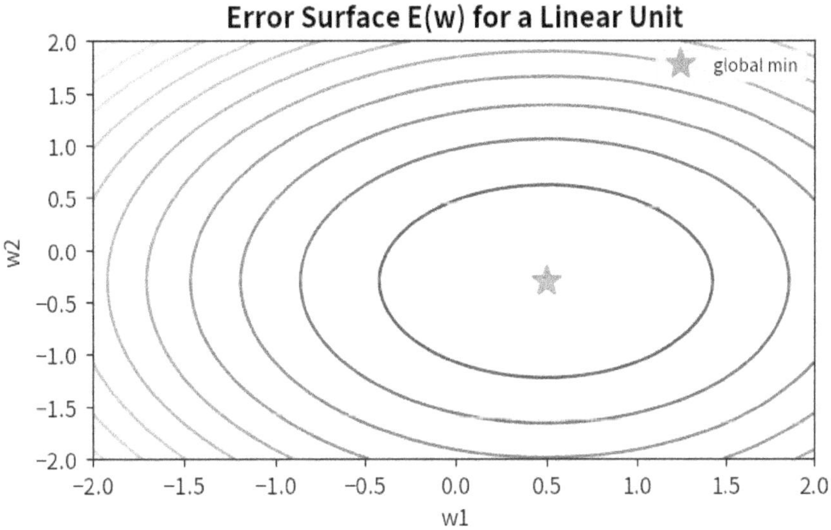

For a sigmoid unit $\sigma(net) = 1/(1+e^{-net})$ the chain rule inserts the extra factor $\sigma'(net) = \sigma(net)(1-\sigma(net))$, giving the logistic-regression update.

Stochastic vs batch gradient descent

• **Batch** – accumulate the gradient over the whole training set, then update once.
• **Stochastic (incremental)** – update after every single example. Faster on large data, noisier trajectory, often escapes shallow local minima.

Python – Delta rule / logistic unit

```
import numpy as np

def sigmoid(z):
    return 1 / (1 + np.exp(-np.clip(z, -40, 40)))

class DeltaRule:
    def __init__(self, n_in, lr=0.5, epochs=2000):
        self.w = np.random.randn(n_in)*0.1
        self.b = 0.0
        self.lr = lr
        self.epochs = epochs
    def predict_proba(self, X):
        return sigmoid(X @ self.w + self.b)
    def fit(self, X, y):
        for _ in range(self.epochs):
            o = self.predict_proba(X)
            err = y - o
            self.w += self.lr * (X.T @ (err * o * (1-o))) / len(y)
            self.b += self.lr * np.mean(err * o * (1-o))
        return self

X = np.array([[0,0],[0,1],[1,0],[1,1]], float)
y = np.array([0.,1.,1.,1.])
model = DeltaRule(2).fit(X, y)
print(np.round(model.predict_proba(X), 3))
```

3.5 MULTILAYER NETWORKS AND BACK-PROPAGATION

A multi-layer perceptron (MLP) stacks several layers of non-linear units. Hidden layers let the network form non-linear decision surfaces and therefore solve problems (e.g. XOR) that a single perceptron cannot.

Two-Layer Feed-forward Network

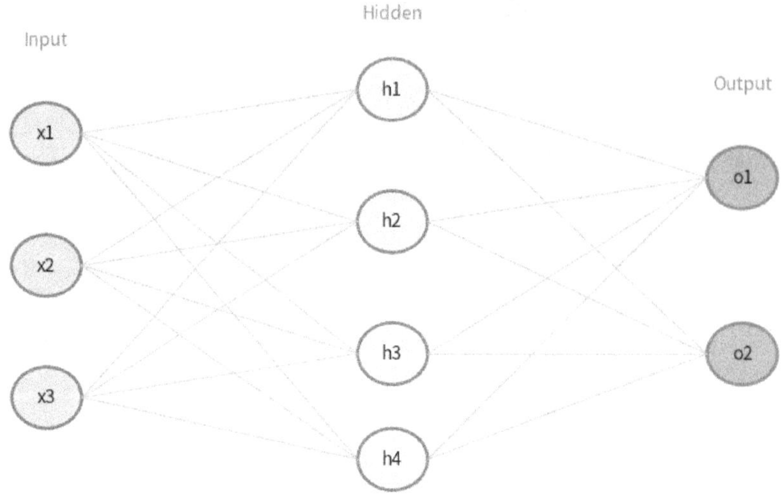

Forward pass

For every unit j compute the net input and the activation:

$$net_j = \Sigma_i\, w_{ji}\, x_{ji}\,,\; o_j = \sigma(net_j)$$

where σ is typically the sigmoid (or tanh / ReLU).

Back-propagation – derivation of the weight updates

We minimise $E = ½\, \Sigma_{k\in \text{outputs}} (t_k - o_k)^2$ by gradient descent. Applying the chain rule yields error terms δ for every unit.

Output unit k

$$\delta_k = (t_k - o_k)\, o_k\, (1 - o_k)$$

Hidden unit h

$$\delta_h = o_h\, (1 - o_h)\, \Sigma_{k\in \text{Downstream}(h)}\, w_{kh}\, \delta_k$$

Weight update for every connection:

$$\Delta w_{ji} = \eta\, \delta_j\, x_{ji}$$

The algorithm therefore consists of a forward pass that computes all activations, followed by a backward pass that propagates the δ's from the output layer back to the input.

Python – Complete back-prop trainer (one hidden layer)

```
import numpy as np

class MLP:
    def __init__(self, n_in, n_hidden, n_out, lr=0.5):
        self.W1 = np.random.randn(n_in, n_hidden)*0.5
        self.b1 = np.zeros((1, n_hidden))
        self.W2 = np.random.randn(n_hidden, n_out)*0.5
        self.b2 = np.zeros((1, n_out))
        self.lr = lr
    def _sig(self, z):
        return 1/(1+np.exp(-np.clip(z,-40,40)))
    def forward(self, X):
        self.a1 = self._sig(X @ self.W1 + self.b1)
        self.a2 = self._sig(self.a1 @ self.W2 + self.b2)
        return self.a2
    def backward(self, X, y):
        m = len(y)
        dz2 = (self.a2 - y) * self.a2 * (1 - self.a2)
        dW2 = self.a1.T @ dz2 / m
        db2 = np.mean(dz2, axis=0, keepdims=True)
        dz1 = (dz2 @ self.W2.T) * self.a1 * (1 - self.a1)
        dW1 = X.T @ dz1 / m
        db1 = np.mean(dz1, axis=0, keepdims=True)
        self.W2 -= self.lr*dW2; self.b2 -= self.lr*db2
        self.W1 -= self.lr*dW1; self.b1 -= self.lr*db1
```

```
    def fit(self, X, y, epochs=5000):
        for _ in range(epochs):
            self.forward(X); self.backward(X, y)
        return self

# XOR
X = np.array([[0,0],[0,1],[1,0],[1,1]], float)
y = np.array([[0],[1],[1],[0]], float)
net = MLP(2, 4, 1, lr=0.7).fit(X, y, epochs=8000)
print("XOR preds:", np.round(net.forward(X).ravel(), 3))
```

The same trainer can be applied to any numeric data set of compatible shape. Adding an L2 weight-decay term (λ■W■^{2}) to the weight update is a simple and effective regulariser.

— End of rewritten §§ 3.4–3.5 —

MODULE 4

BAYESIAN LEARNING

Expanded rewrite with full derivations, diagrams and runnable Python. Covers Bayes' theorem, MAP & ML, Brute-Force MAP learning, Naïve Bayes, Bayesian networks and MDL.

1. Bayes' Theorem – Derivation and Meaning

Bayesian reasoning treats hypotheses as random variables. Let *h* be a hypothesis and *D* the observed data. From the definition of conditional probability:

$$P(h \wedge D) = P(h|D)\,P(D) = P(D|h)\,P(h)$$

Rearranging immediately yields Bayes' theorem:

$$\mathbf{P(h|D) = P(D|h)\,P(h)\,/\,P(D)}$$

- **P(h)** – prior (belief before seeing data)
- **P(D|h)** – likelihood (how well h explains D)
- **P(D)** – evidence / marginal likelihood (normaliser)
- **P(h|D)** – posterior (belief after seeing data)

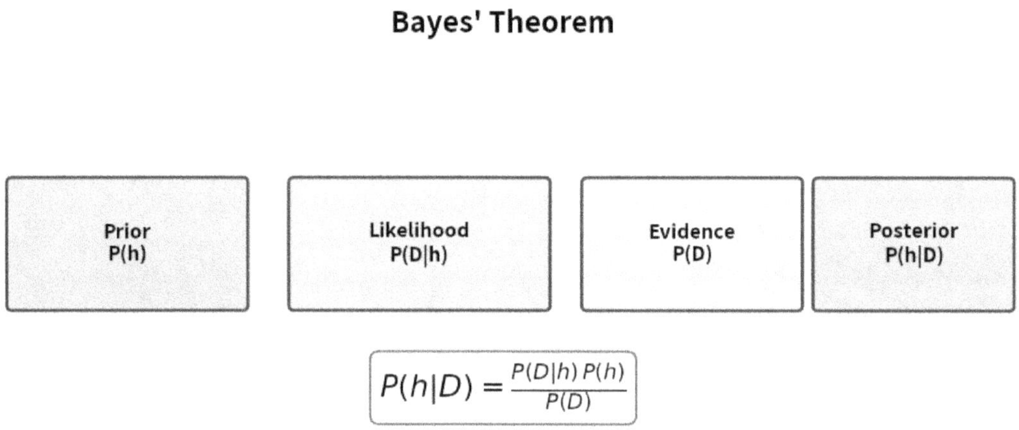

Medical diagnosis example (classic derivation)

Let C = patient has cancer, ¬C = no cancer. Lab test returns + or –.
Given: P(C)=0.008, P(+|C)=0.98, P(+|¬C)=0.03.
We want P(C|+).

$P(C|+) = P(+|C)P(C) / P(+)$, $P(+) = P(+|C)P(C) + P(+|\neg C)P(\neg C)$
$= (0.98 \cdot 0.008) / (0.98 \cdot 0.008 + 0.03 \cdot 0.992) \approx 0.00784 / 0.0376 \approx 0.21$

Even after a positive test the posterior is only ≈21 % because the disease is rare. This illustrates how strongly the prior influences the posterior.

2. Maximum a Posteriori (MAP) and Maximum Likelihood (ML)

In learning we usually seek a single best hypothesis. Two common criteria:

MAP vs Maximum Likelihood

Maximum a Posteriori (MAP)	Maximum Likelihood (ML)
$h_{MAP} = \arg\max_h P(D\|h)P(h)$	$h_{ML} = \arg\max_h P(D\|h)$
uses prior knowledge P(h)	uniform prior → MAP reduces to ML

Derivation of the MAP rule

h_{MAP} = arg $\max_h$ P(h|D) = arg $\max_h$ P(D|h)P(h)/P(D)
Because P(D) does not depend on h it can be dropped:
h_{MAP} = arg $\max_h$ P(D|h) P(h)
When the prior is uniform, P(h) is constant and MAP reduces to the maximum-likelihood hypothesis h_{ML} = arg $\max_h$ P(D|h).

Python – Computing MAP for a coin-bias hypothesis space

```
import numpy as np

hyps  = {'h1': 0.3, 'h2': 0.5, 'h3': 0.8}    # possible P(Heads)
prior = {'h1': 0.2, 'h2': 0.5, 'h3': 0.3}
data  = ['H','H','H','T']

def likelihood(theta, data):
    return np.prod([theta if d=='H' else 1-theta for d in data])

post = {h: likelihood(th, data)*prior[h] for h,th in hyps.items()}
Z = sum(post.values())
post = {h: v/Z for h,v in post.items()}
print("Posteriors:", {h: round(p,3) for h,p in post.items()})
print("MAP hypothesis:", max(post, key=post.get))
```

3. Brute-Force MAP Learning Algorithm

For a finite hypothesis space H the MAP hypothesis can be found by enumerating every h ∈ H, computing the posterior, and selecting the maximum. Under the assumptions

- every hypothesis is equally likely a priori, P(h) = 1/|H|
- data are noise-free, P(D|h) = 1 if h is consistent with D, else 0

the posterior is uniform over the version space $VS_{H,D}$ and zero elsewhere. Consequently every consistent hypothesis is a MAP hypothesis.

4. Naïve Bayes Classifier – Full Derivation

We want the most probable target value given attribute vector ■a1…an■:

$$v_{MAP} = \arg\max_{vj} P(vj \mid a1\ldots an) = \arg\max_{vj} P(a1\ldots an \mid vj)\, P(vj) / P(a1\ldots an)$$

The denominator is independent of vj. The naïve Bayes assumption states that the attributes are conditionally independent given the class:

$$P(a1\ldots an \mid vj) = \Pi_i P(ai \mid vj)$$

Substituting yields the practical decision rule:

$$\mathbf{v_{NB} = \arg\max_{vj} P(vj)\, \Pi_i P(ai \mid vj)}$$

Naive Bayes Classifier Structure

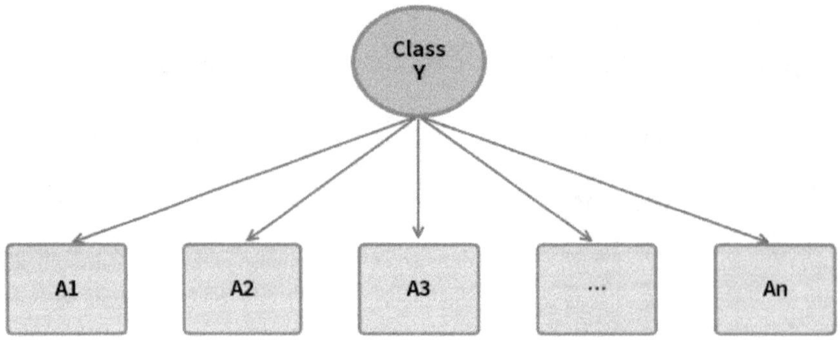

Assumption: features conditionally independent given the class

Python – Complete Laplace-smoothed Naïve Bayes (Play-Tennis)

```
from collections import defaultdict
import math

data = [
    ("Sunny","Hot","High","Weak","No"), ("Sunny","Hot","High","Strong","No"),
    ("Overcast","Hot","High","Weak","Yes"), ("Rain","Mild","High","Weak","Yes"),
    ("Rain","Cool","Normal","Weak","Yes"), ("Rain","Cool","Normal","Strong","No"),
    ("Overcast","Cool","Normal","Strong","Yes"), ("Sunny","Mild","High","Weak","No"),
    ("Sunny","Cool","Normal","Weak","Yes"), ("Rain","Mild","Normal","Weak","Yes"),
    ("Sunny","Mild","Normal","Strong","Yes"), ("Overcast","Mild","High","Strong","Yes"),
    ("Overcast","Hot","Normal","Weak","Yes"), ("Rain","Mild","High","Strong","No"),
]

def train(data, alpha=1.0):
    class_cnt = defaultdict(int)
    feat_cnt  = defaultdict(lambda: defaultdict(lambda: defaultdict(int)))
    for *xs, y in data:
        class_cnt[y] += 1
        for i,v in enumerate(xs):
            feat_cnt[i][v][y] += 1
    return class_cnt, feat_cnt

def predict(class_cnt, feat_cnt, x, alpha=1.0, n_vals=(3,3,2,2)):
    total = sum(class_cnt.values())
    scores = {}
    for c, cnt in class_cnt.items():
        logp = math.log((cnt+alpha)/(total+alpha*len(class_cnt)))
        for i,v in enumerate(x):
            logp += math.log((feat_cnt[i][v][c]+alpha)/(cnt+alpha*n_vals[i]))
        scores[c] = logp
    return max(scores, key=scores.get), scores

cc, fc = train(data)
label, scores = predict(cc, fc, ("Sunny","Cool","High","Strong"))
print("Predicted:", label)
print("Log-scores:", {k: round(v,3) for k,v in scores.items()})
```

5. Bayesian Networks

A Bayesian network is a directed acyclic graph (DAG) that encodes a joint probability distribution by a set of conditional independence assumptions. The joint factorises as:

$$P(X1\ldots Xn) = \Pi_i\, P(Xi \mid Parents(Xi))$$

Example Bayesian Network (Alarm)

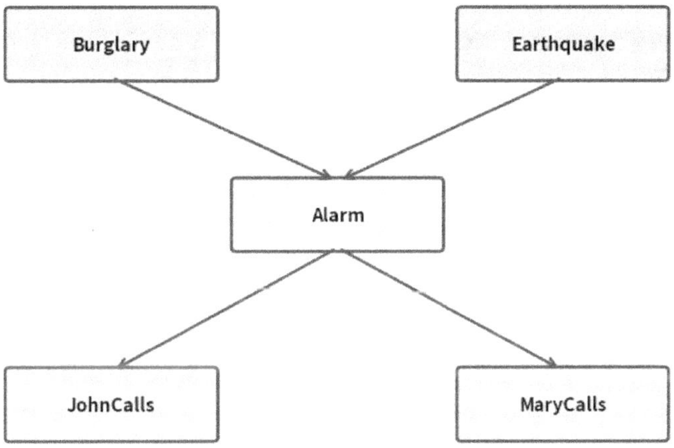

Each node stores a Conditional Probability Table (CPT) given its parents. Exact inference can be performed by variable elimination or belief propagation; for large networks approximate methods (MCMC, variational inference) are used.

Python – Exact inference by enumeration on the Alarm network

```
P_B, P_E = 0.001, 0.002
P_A = {(True,True):0.95,(True,False):0.94,(False,True):0.29,(False,False):0.001}
P_J = {True:0.90, False:0.05}

def joint(b, e, a, j):
    return (P_B if b else 1-P_B)*(P_E if e else 1-P_E)*P_A[(b,e)]*(P_J[a] if j else 1-P_J[a])

num = sum(joint(True,e,a,True) for e in [True,False] for a in [True,False])
den = sum(joint(b,e,a,True) for b in [True,False] for e in [True,False] for a in [True,False])
print(f"P(Burglary | JohnCalls) ≈ {num/den:.4f}")
```

6. Minimum Description Length (MDL) Principle

Occam's razor formalised with information theory: choose the hypothesis that minimises the total number of bits needed to describe the hypothesis plus the data given the hypothesis:

$$h_{MDL} = \arg\min_h \left(L_{C1}(h) + L_{C2}(D|h) \right)$$

Under a suitable choice of codes this is exactly equivalent to the MAP hypothesis (because $-\log_2 P(h)$ is the optimal code length for h). MDL therefore automatically balances model complexity against data fit and is a principled defence against over-fitting.

7. Selected VTU-style Questions (answered)

Q1. State Bayes' theorem and explain each term with a worked example. (6 M)

Section 1 + medical-diagnosis derivation.

Q2. Distinguish MAP and ML. When do they coincide? (6 M)

Section 2 + the comparison diagram.

Q3. Derive the Naïve Bayes decision rule and apply it to a data set. (10 M)

Section 4 contains the full derivation, structural diagram and a complete Python implementation.

Q4. What is a Bayesian network? Give the factorisation and an inference example. (8 M)

Section 5 + Alarm network diagram + enumeration program.

— End of expanded Module 4 — All programs run with pure Python / NumPy.

MODULE 5

EVALUATING HYPOTHESES · INSTANCE-BASED LEARNING · REINFORCEMENT LEARNING

Fully rewritten with diagrams and runnable Python. Covers hypothesis accuracy & confidence intervals, k-Nearest Neighbours, and Q-learning with a grid-world demo.

1. Evaluating Hypothesis Accuracy

After learning a hypothesis *h* we need an estimate of its true error on the whole instance space. We draw a test sample of size *n* and count the number of mistakes *r*. The observed error is $\mathbf{error_S(h) = r/n}$.

Under the binomial model the number of errors follows Binomial(*n*, $error_D(h)$). A normal approximation yields a confidence interval:

$error_D(h) \in error_S(h) \pm z_c \sqrt{(error_S(1-error_S)/n)}$

where $z_c = 1.96$ for a 95 % interval (large *n*).

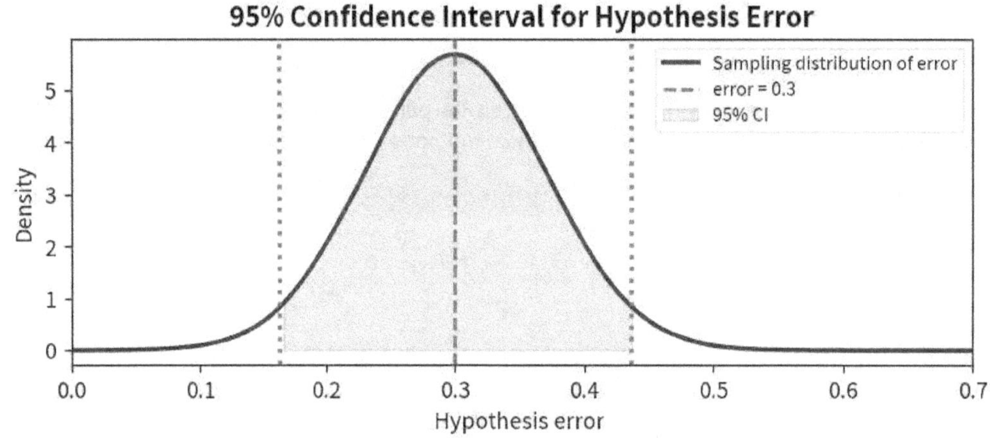

Python – Confidence interval for hypothesis error

```
import math

def confidence_interval(r, n, z=1.96):
    """r = number of errors, n = test-set size"""
    p = r / n
    se = math.sqrt(p * (1 - p) / n)
    return p - z * se, p + z * se

# Example: 12 errors on 100 test examples
lo, hi = confidence_interval(12, 100)
print(f"Observed error = 0.12")
print(f"95% CI ≈ [{lo:.3f}, {hi:.3f}]")
```

2. Instance-Based Learning – k-Nearest Neighbours

Instance-based methods store the training examples and delay generalisation until a query arrives. The most popular algorithm is **k-Nearest Neighbours (k-NN)**:

1. Given query x_q, find the k training instances closest to x_q (usually Euclidean distance).
2. For classification return the majority class among those k neighbours.
3. For regression return the average of the k target values.

1-NN produces a Voronoi tessellation of the instance space; larger k yields smoother decision boundaries but can also smooth away genuine structure.

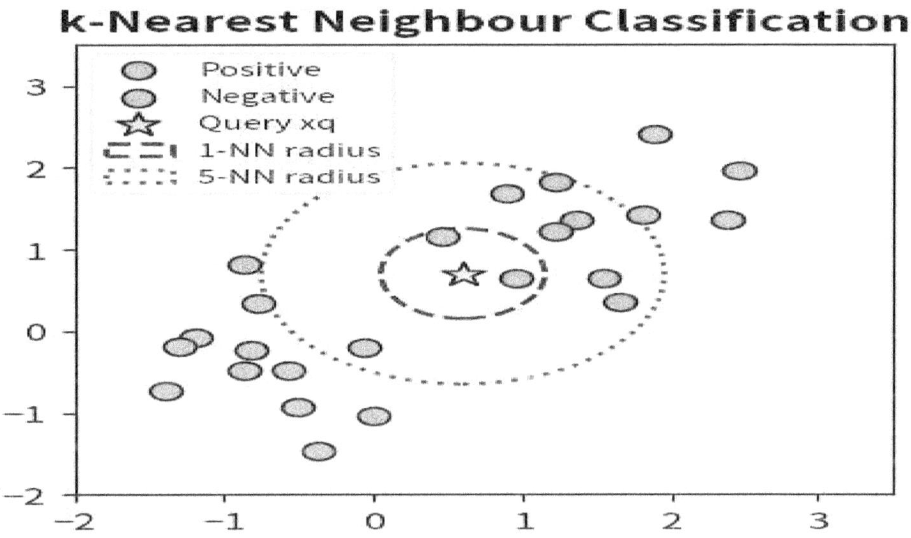

Python – k-NN classifier from scratch

```
import numpy as np
from collections import Counter

class KNN:
    def __init__(self, k=3):
        self.k = k
    def fit(self, X, y):
        self.X, self.y = np.asarray(X, float), np.asarray(y)
        return self
    def predict(self, Xq):
        Xq = np.atleast_2d(Xq)
        preds = []
        for q in Xq:
            dists = np.linalg.norm(self.X - q, axis=1)
            idx = np.argsort(dists)[:self.k]
            preds.append(Counter(self.y[idx]).most_common(1)[0][0])
        return np.array(preds)

# Tiny demo
X = [[1,2],[2,3],[3,1],[6,5],[7,7],[8,6]]
y = [0,0,0,1,1,1]
clf = KNN(k=3).fit(X, y)
print("Prediction for [4,4]:", clf.predict([[4,4]])[0])
print("Prediction for [7,5]:", clf.predict([[7,5]])[0])
```

3. Reinforcement Learning & Q-Learning

In reinforcement learning an agent interacts with an environment by taking actions and receiving rewards. The goal is to learn a policy that maximises expected cumulative reward.

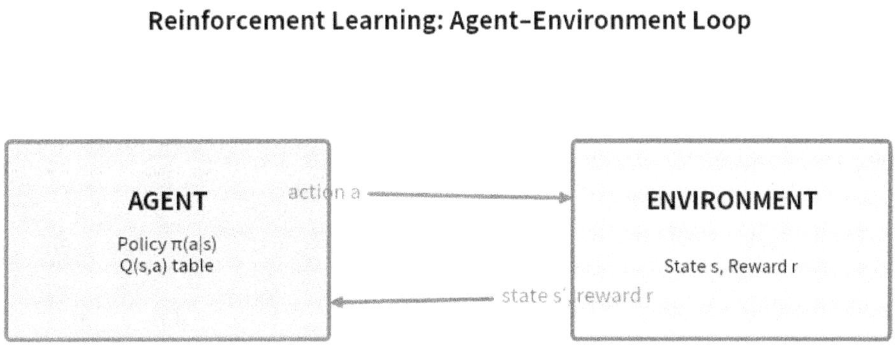

Q-learning is a model-free off-policy algorithm that learns the action-value function Q(s,a). The update rule is:

$Q(s,a) \leftarrow Q(s,a) + \alpha\,[\,r + \gamma \max_{a'} Q(s',a') - Q(s,a)\,]$

where α is the learning rate and γ the discount factor. Under standard conditions Q-learning converges to the optimal Q^* for any exploration policy that visits every state-action pair infinitely often.

Simple Grid-World (Q-learning demo)

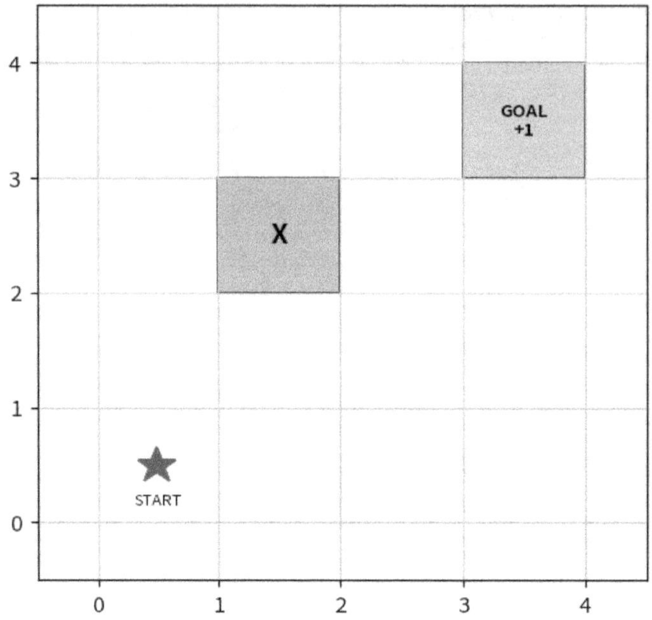

Python – Q-learning on a tiny grid-world

```
import numpy as np

# 4x4 grid, goal at (3,3), obstacle at (1,2)
n = 4
actions = [(0,1),(0,-1),(1,0),(-1,0)]  # N S E W
Q = np.zeros((n, n, 4))
alpha, gamma, eps = 0.3, 0.9, 0.2
goal = (3, 3)
obstacle = (1, 2)

def step(s, a):
    ns = (s[0] + actions[a][0], s[1] + actions[a][1])
    if not (0 <= ns[0] < n and 0 <= ns[1] < n) or ns == obstacle:
        return s, -0.1
    if ns == goal:
        return ns, +1.0
    return ns, -0.01

for episode in range(800):
    s = (0, 0)
    while s != goal:
        if np.random.rand() < eps:
            a = np.random.randint(4)
        else:
            a = np.argmax(Q[s[0], s[1]])
        ns, r = step(s, a)
        Q[s[0], s[1], a] += alpha * (r + gamma * np.max(Q[ns[0], ns[1]]) - Q[s[0], s[1], a])
        s = ns

s = (0, 0)
path = [s]
for _ in range(20):
    if s == goal: break
    a = np.argmax(Q[s[0], s[1]])
    s, _ = step(s, a)
    path.append(s)
print("Learned path:", path)
print("Q-values at start:", np.round(Q[0,0], 2))
```

4. Selected VTU-style Questions (answered)

Q1. How do you estimate the accuracy of a hypothesis? Derive a confidence interval. (8 M)

Section 1 + the binomial / normal-approximation formula and the Python helper.

Q2. Explain the k-Nearest Neighbour algorithm with a diagram. (6 M)

Section 2 contains the algorithm, a visual illustration, and a complete implementation.

Q3. Write the Q-learning update rule and illustrate with a simple example. (8 M)

Section 3 gives the update, the agent–environment diagram, a grid-world figure, and a full Q-learning program that learns a path to the goal.

— End of rewritten Module 5 — All code runs with pure Python / NumPy.

Exercise Solving Modules

The following pages contain solved and partially-solved examination-style questions organised by topic. They correspond to the five traditional VTU modules and are intended for practice and revision.

Exercise Module 1 – Introduction & Concept Learning
Exercise Module 2 – Decision Trees / ID3
Exercise Module 3 – Artificial Neural Networks
Exercise Module 4 – Bayesian Learning
Exercise Module 5 – Evaluating Hypotheses, Instance-based Learning & Reinforcement Learning

Note: The main theoretical treatment of Modules 3–5 (with full derivations, diagrams and Python implementations) appears earlier in the notes (pages 90–103).

MODULE 1

INTRODUCTION, CONCEPT LEARNING

1. Specify the learning task for "A Checkers learning problem". (3M)(JAN 19)

Checkers game: A computer program that learns to play ***checkers*** might improve its performance as measured by its ability to win at the class of tasks involving playing checkers games, through experience obtained by playing games against self.

***A checkers learning problem*:**

- Task T: playing checkers
- Performance measure P: percent of games won against opponents
- Training experience E: playing practice games against itself

[The target function to learn is to **choose a legal move**, the most obvious choice for the type of information to be learned is a program, or function, that chooses the best move for any given board state.

$$ChooseMove : B \rightarrow M$$

which indicate that this function accepts as input any board from the set of legal board states B and produces as output some move from the set of legal moves M

ChooseMove is a choice for the target function in checkers example, but this function will turn out to be very difficult to learn given the kind of indirect training experience available to our system]

2. Discuss the following with respect to the above

a. Choosing the training experience

b. Choosing the target function

c. Choosing a function approximation algorithm. (9M)(JAN 19)

i. Whether the training experience provides ***direct or indirect feedback*** regarding the choices made by the performance system.

In checkers' game, in learning to play checkers, the system might learn from ***direct training examples*** consisting of ***individual checkers board states*** and ***the correct move for each***

ii. The degree to which the ***learner controls the sequence of training examples***

In checkers game, the learner might depend on the ***teacher*** to select informative board states and to provide the correct move for each.

Alternatively, the learner might itself propose board states that it finds particularly confusing and ask the teacher for the correct move.

iii. How well it represents the ***distribution of examples*** over which the final system performance P must be measured
In checkers game, the performance metric P is the percent of games the system wins in the world tournament

Choosing the Target Function

Task → what type of knowledge will be learned and how this will be used by the performance program

Consider a checkers-playing program that can generate the legal moves from any board state.

The program needs only to learn how to choose the best move from among these legal moves → the most obvious choice for the type of information to be learned is a program, or function, that chooses the best move for any given board state.

Let ***ChooseMove*** be the target function and the notation is

$$\textbf{\textit{ChooseMove}} : B \rightarrow M$$

This function accepts as input any board from the set of legal board states B and produces as output some move from the set of legal moves M.

Alternative Target Function → evaluation function → assign numerical score to any given board state

$$V: B \rightarrow R$$

which denote that V maps any legal board state from the set B to some real value. Example, in checkers game,

- If b is a final board state that is won, then V(b) = 100
- If b is a final board state that is lost, then V(b) = -100
- If b is a final board state that is drawn, then V(b) = 0
- If b is a not a final state in the game, then V(b) = V(b')

b' is the best final board state that can be achieved starting from b

Choosing a Function Approximation Algorithm

In order to learn the target function **f** we require a set of training examples, each describing a specific board state b and the training value Vtrain(b) for b. Each training example is an ordered pair of the form (b, Vtrain(b)).

The following training example describes a board state b in which black has won the game (note x2 = 0 indicates that red has no remaining pieces) and for which the target function value Vtrain(b) is therefore +100.

((x1=3, x2=0, x3=1, x4=0, x5=0, x6=0), +100)

Function Approximation Procedure

- Derive training examples from the indirect training experience available to the learner

  A simple approach for estimating training values for intermediate board states is to assign the training value of Vtrain(b) foR any intermediate board state b to bê V(Successor(b))

  Vtrain(b) ← V (Successor(b))

- Adjusts the weights wi to best fit these training examples

  Specify the learning algorithm for choosing the weights wi to best fit the set of training examples {(b, Vtrain(b))}

$$E \equiv \sum_{\langle b, V_{train}(b)\rangle \in \text{ training examples}} (V_{train}(b) - \hat{V}(b))^2$$

3. Comment on the issue in machine learning (4M)(JAN 19)

Issues in Machine Learning

The field of machine learning, and much of this book, is concerned with answering questions such as the following

- What algorithms exist for learning general target functions from specific training examples? In what settings will particular algorithms converge to the desired function, given sufficient training data? Which algorithms perform best for which types of problems and representations?
- How much training data is sufficient? What general bounds can be found to relate the confidence in learned hypotheses to the amount of training experience and the character of the learner's hypothesis space?
- When and how can prior knowledge held by the learner guide the process of generalizing from examples? Can prior knowledge be helpful even when it is only approximately correct?
- What is the best strategy for choosing a useful next training experience, and how does the choice of this strategy alter the complexity of the learning problem?
- What is the best way to reduce the learning task to one or more function approximation problems? Put another way, what specific functions should the system attempt to learn? Can this process itself be automated?
- How can the learner automatically alter its representation to improve its ability to represent and learn the target function?

4. Write candidate elimination algorithm. Apply the algorithm to obtain the final version space for the training example,

Sl. No.	Sky	AirTemp	Humidity	Wind	Water	Forecast	EnjoySport
1	Sunny	Warm	Normal	Strong	Warm	Same	Yes
2	Sunny	Warm	High	Strong	Warm	Same	Yes
3	Rainy	Cool	High	Strong	Warm	Change	No
4	Sunny	Warm	High	Strong	Cool	Change	Yes

(10M) (JAN 19)

https://youtu.be/40D3G_cCtWc

CANDIDATE-ELIMINTION algorithm begins by initializing the version space to the set of all hypotheses in H;

Initializing the G boundary set to contain the most general hypothesis in H

G0 <?, ?, ?, ?, ?, ?>

Initializing the S boundary set to contain the most specific (least general) hypothesis S0

S_0

- When the first training example is presented, the CANDIDATE-ELIMINTION algorithm checks the S boundary and finds that it is overly specific and it fails to cover the positive example.
- The boundary is therefore revised by moving it to the least more general hypothesis that covers this new example
- No update of the G boundary is needed in response to this training example because Go correctly covers this example

For training example d,

⟨Sunny, Warm, Normal, Strong, Warm, Same⟩ +

S_0 ⟨∅, ∅, ∅, ∅, ∅. ∅⟩

S_1 ⟨*Sunny, Warm, Normal, Strong, Warm, Same*⟩

G_0, G_1 ⟨?, ?, ?, ?, ?, ?⟩

- When the second training example is observed, it has a similar effect of generalizing S further to S2, leaving G again unchanged i.e., G2 = G1 = G0

For training example d,
⟨Sunny, Warm, High, Strong, Warm, Same⟩ +

S_1 ⟨Sunny, Warm, Normal, Strong, Warm, Same⟩

S_2 ⟨Sunny, Warm, ?, Strong, Warm, Same⟩

G_1, G_2 ⟨?, ?, ?, ?, ?, ?⟩

- Consider the third training example. This negative example reveals that the G boundary of the version space is overly general, that is, the hypothesis in G incorrectly predicts that this new example is a positive example.
- The hypothesis in the G boundary must therefore be specialized until it correctly classifies this new negative example

For training example d,
⟨Rainy, Cold, High, Strong, Warm, Change ⟩ –

S_2, S_3 ⟨Sunny, Warm, ?, Strong, Warm, Same⟩

G_3 ⟨Sunny, ?, ?, ?, ?, ?⟩ ⟨?, Warm, ?, ?, ?, ?⟩ ⟨?, ?, ?, ?, ?, Same⟩

G_2 ⟨?, ?, ?, ?, ?, ?⟩

Given that there are six attributes that could be specified to specialize G2, why are there only three new hypotheses in G3?

For example, the hypothesis h = (?, ?, Normal, ?, ?, ?) is a minimal specialization of G2 that correctly labels the new example as a negative example, but it is not included in G3. The reason this hypothesis is excluded is that it is inconsistent with the previously encountered positive examples

- Consider the fourth training example.

For training example d,
⟨Sunny, Warm, High, Strong, Cool Change ⟩ +

S_3 ⟨Sunny, Warm, ?, Strong, Warm, Same⟩

S_4 ⟨Sunny, Warm, ?, Strong, ?, ?⟩

G_4 ⟨Sunny, ?, ?, ?, ?, ?⟩ ⟨?, Warm, ?, ?, ?, ?⟩

G_3 ⟨Sunny, ?, ?, ?, ?, ?⟩ ⟨?, Warm, ?, ?, ?, ?⟩ ⟨?, ?, ?, ?, ?, Same⟩

- This positive example further generalizes the S boundary of the version space. It also results in removing one member of the G boundary, because this member fails to cover the new positive example
- After processing these four examples, the boundary sets S4 and G4 delimit the version space of all hypotheses consistent with the set of incrementally observed training examples

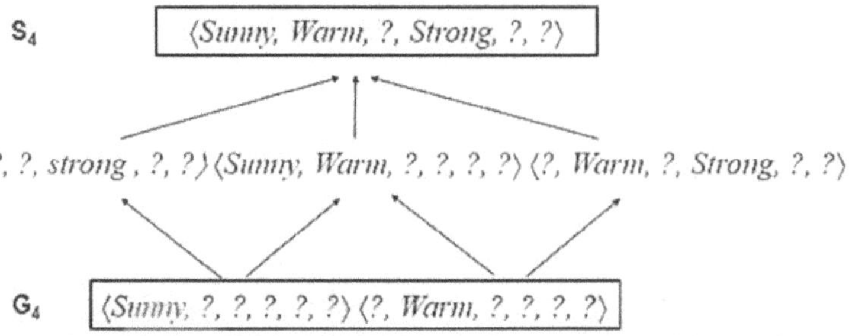

5. Discuss about an unbiased learner.(6M) (JAN 19)

- The solution to the problem of assuring that the target concept is in the hypothesis space H is to provide a hypothesis space capable of representing every teachable concept that is representing every possible subset of the instances X.
- The set of all subsets of a set X is called the power set of X
- In the ***EnjoySport*** learning task the size of the instance space X of days described by the six attributes is 96 instances.
- Thus, there are 2^{96} distinct target concepts that could be defined over this instance space and learner might be called upon to learn.
- The conjunctive hypothesis space is able to represent only 973 of these - a biased hypothesis space indeed
- Let us reformulate the ***EnjoySport*** learning task in an unbiased way by defining a new hypothesis space H' that can represent every subset of instances
- The target concept "Sky = Sunny or Sky = Cloudy" could then be described as (Sunny, ?, ?, ?, ?, ?) ∨ (Cloudy, ?, ?, ?, ?, ?)

6. Define machine learning. Describe the steps in designing learning system. (8M)(JULY 19)

Definition:

Machine learning is a field where a computer program is said to learn from experience E with respect to some class of tasks T and performance measure P, if its performance at tasks in T, as measured by P, improves with experience E.

Designing learning system

The steps in designing a learning system are:

i. *Choosing the Training Experience*

REFER QUESTION - 2

ii. *Choosing the Target Function*

REFER QUESTION - 2

iii. *Choosing a Representation for the Target Function*

Let's choose a simple representation - for any given board state, the function ***c*** will be calculated as a linear combination of the following board features:

- xl: the number of black pieces on the board
- x2: the number of red pieces on the board
- x3: the number of black kings on the board
- x4: the number of red kings on the board
- x5: the number of black pieces threatened by red (i.e., which can be captured on red's next turn)
- x6: the number of red pieces threatened by black

Thus, learning program will represent as a linear function of the form

$$\hat{V}(b) = w_0 + w_1x_1 + w_2x_2 + w_3x_3 + w_4x_4 + w_5x_5 + w_6x_6$$

Where,

- w0 through w6 are numerical coefficients, or weights, to be chosen by the learning algorithm.
- Learned values for the weights w1 through w6 will determine the relative importance of the various board features in determining the value of the board
- The weight w0 will provide an additive constant to the board value

iv. *Choosing a Function Approximation Algorithm*

- o Estimating training values
- o Adjusting the weights

REFER QUESTION - 2

v. *The Final Design*

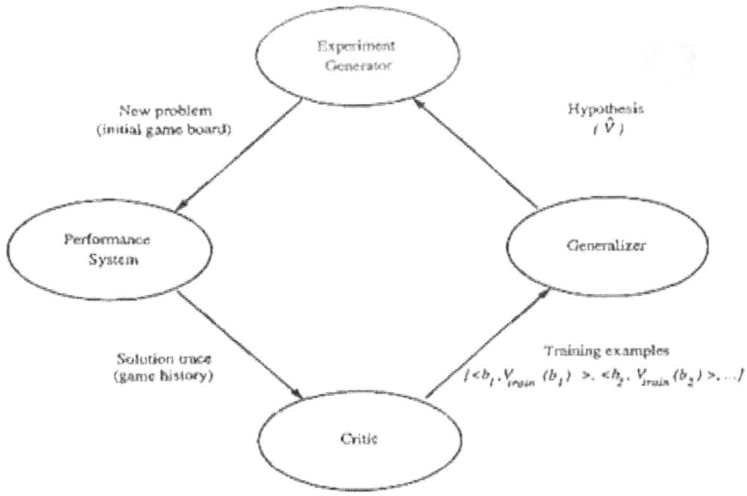

a) **The Performance System** is the module that must solve the given performance task by using the learned target function(s). It takes an instance of a new problem (new game) as input and produces a trace of its solution (game history) as output.

b) **The Critic** takes as input the history or trace of the game and produces as output a set of training examples of the target function

c) **The Generalizer** takes as input the training examples and produces an output hypothesis that is its estimate of the target function. It generalizes from the specific training examples, hypothesizing a general function that covers these examples and other cases beyond the training examples.

d) **The Experiment Generator** takes as input the current hypothesis and outputs a new problem (i.e., initial board state) for the Performance System to explore. Its role is to pick new practice problems that will maximize the learning rate of the overall system.

7. Write Find-S algorithm and explain with example. (4m) (JULY 19)

FIND-S Algorithm

1. Initialize *h* to the most specific hypothesis in *H*
2. For each positive training instance *x*
    For each attribute constraint a_i in *h*
        If the constraint a_i is satisfied by *x*
            Then do nothing
        Else replace a_i in *h* by the next more general constraint that is satisfied by *x*.
        Output hypothesis *h*

Example,

To illustrate this algorithm, assume the learner is given the sequence of training examples from the ***EnjoySport*** task

Example	Sky	AirTemp	Humidity	Wind	Water	Forecast	EnjoySport
1	Sunny	Warm	Normal	Strong	Warm	Same	Yes
2	Sunny	Warm	High	Strong	Warm	Same	Yes
3	Rainy	Cold	High	Strong	Warm	Change	No
4	Sunny	Warm	High	Strong	Cool	Change	Yes

- The first step of FIND-S is to initialize h to the most specific hypothesis in H h - (Ø, Ø, Ø, Ø, Ø, Ø)
- Consider the first training example
    x1 = <Sunny Warm Normal Strong Warm Same>, +

Observing the first training example, it is clear that hypothesis *h* is too specific. None of the "Ø" constraints in h are satisfied by this example, so each is replaced by the next *more general constraint* that fits the example

h1 = <Sunny Warm Normal Strong Warm Same>

- Consider the second training example
  x2 = <Sunny, Warm, High, Strong, Warm, Same>, +

The second training example forces the algorithm to further generalize h, this time substituting a "?" in place of any attribute value in h that is not satisfied by the new example

h2 = <Sunny Warm ? Strong Warm Same>

- Consider the third training example
  x3 = <Rainy, Cold, High, Strong, Warm, Change>, -

Upon encountering the third training the algorithm makes no change to h. The FIND-S algorithm simply ignores every negative example.

h3 = < Sunny Warm ? Strong Warm Same>

- Consider the fourth training example
  x4 = <Sunny Warm High Strong Cool Change>, +

- The fourth example leads to a further generalization of h h4 = < Sunny Warm ? Strong ? ? >

8. Explain List-then-eliminate algorithm. (4M) (JULY 19)

The LIST-THEN-ELIMINATION algorithm
The LIST-THEN-ELIMINATE algorithm first initializes the version space to contain all hypotheses in H and then eliminates any hypothesis found inconsistent with any training example

---

1. ***VersionSpace c*** a list containing every hypothesis in H
2. For each training example, (x, c(x))
   remove from ***VersionSpace*** any hypothesis h for which h(x) ≠ c(x)
3. Output the list of hypotheses in ***VersionSpace***

- List-Then-Eliminate works in principle, so long as version space is finite.
- However, since it requires exhaustive enumeration of all hypotheses in practice it is not feasible

9. List out any 5 applications of machine learning. (5M) (JULY 19)

i. ***A checkers learning problem*:**
   Task T: playing checkers
   Performance measure P: percent of games won against opponents

Training experience E: playing practice games against itself

ii. ***A handwriting recognition learning problem:***

- Task T: recognizing and classifying handwritten words within images
- Performance measure P: percent of words correctly classified
- Training experience E: a database of handwritten words with given classifications

iii. ***A robot driving learning problem*:**

- Task T: driving on public four-lane highways using vision sensors
- Performance measure P: average distance travelled before an error (as judged by human overseer)
- Training experience E: a sequence of images and steering commands recorded while observing a human driver

iv. Learning to recognize spoken words

- Task T: recognizing the spoken words
- Performance measure P: number of recognized words before giving a wrong recognition.
- Training experience E: a sequence of words spoken by a training observer

v. Learning to classify new astronomical structures

- Task T: Classifying astronomical structures
- Performance measure P: number of true classifications before a misclassification of astronomical structure.
- Training experience E: a sequence of dimensions of astronomical structures.

10. What do you mean by hypothesis space, instance space, and version space? (3M) (JULY 19)

Hypothesis space:

The symbol ***H*** to denote the set of all possible hypotheses that the learner may consider regarding the identity of the target concept. Each hypothesis ***h*** in ***H*** represents a Boolean-valued function defined over ***X.***

$$h: X \rightarrow \{0,1\}$$

Instance space:

The set of items over which the concept is defined is called the ***set of instances***, which is denoted by X. **:** X is the set of all possible days, each represented by the attributes.

The concept or function to be learned is called the ***target concept***, which is denoted by c. c can be any Boolean valued function defined over the instances X.

$$c: X \rightarrow \{0,1\}$$

Version space:

The **version space,** denoted $VS_{H,D}$ with respect to hypothesis space ***H*** and training examples D, is the subset of hypotheses from ***H*** consistent with the training examples in D $VS_{H,D}$ $\{h \quad H \mid Consistent\ (h, D)\}$

11. Find the maximally general hypothesis and maximally specific hypothesis for the training examples given in the table using candidate elimination algorithm.

Sl. No.	Sky	AirTemp	Humidity	Wind	Water	Forecast	EnjoySport
1	Sunny	Warm	Normal	Strong	Warm	Same	Yes
2	Sunny	Warm	High	Strong	Warm	Same	Yes
3	Rainy	Cool	High	Strong	Warm	Change	No
4	Sunny	Warm	High	Strong	Cool	Change	Yes

(10M) (JAN 19)

https://youtu.be/40D3G_cCtWc

12. What do you mean by well-posed learning problem? Explain with example. (4M) (JAN 2020)

REFER QUESTION – 6&1

13. Explain the various stages involved in designing a learning system in brief. (8M) (JAN 2020)

REFER QUESTION - 2

14. Write the Find_S algorithm and discuss the issues with the algorithm. (4M) (JAN 2020)

Find_S Algorithm

REFER QUESTION – 7

Issues in Find_S algorithm

Find_S considers only positive examples. These is a possibility that the negative examples also may provide additional proof to obtain maximally specific hypothesis.

Find_S does not answer the questions about

- Whether the learner converged to the correct target concept.
- Need to prefer most specific hypothesis
- Whether the training examples are consistent
- The possibility of having more than one maximally specific consistent hypothesis.

15. List the issues in machine learning. (4M) (JAN 2020)

REFER QUESTION - 3

16. Consider the given below training example which finds malignant tumors from MRI scans.

Example	Shape	Size	Color	Surface	Thickness	Target_Concept
1	Circular	Large	Light	Smooth	Thick	Malignant
2	Circular	Large	Light	Irregular	Thick	Malignant
3	Oval	Large	Dark	Smooth	Thin	Benign
4	Oval	Large	Light	Irregular	Thick	Malignant
5	Circular	Small	Light	Smooth	Thick	Benign

Show the specific and general boundaries of the version space after applying candidate elimination algorithm.

(8M) (JAN 2020)

REFER QP PROBLEM SOLUTIONS

17. Explain the concept of inductive bias in brief. (4M) (JAN 2020)

Inductive bias represents the way that an algorithm is biased towards making an assumption using a hypothesis. The fundamental questions about inductive bias are examined in terms or candidate elimination algorithm.

Biased Learner

Suppose the target concept is not contained in the hypothesis space *H,* then obvious solution is to enrich the hypothesis space to include every possible hypothesis.

For example, in *EnjoySport* example the hypothesis space is restricted to include only conjunctions of attribute values. Therefore, the hypothesis cannot represent even simple disjunctive target concepts such as

"*Sky* = *Sunny* or *Sky* = *Cloudy*"

Once an attribute allows two values, the hypothesis sets the attribute to '?', which means any value is acceptable.

In case there is an example which has 'No' as the outcome for "*Sky* = *Rainy*", the hypothesis incorrectly covers such examples.

Unbiased Learner

The solution to the problem of assuring that the target concept is in the hypothesis space H is to provide a hypothesis space capable of representing every teachable concept that is representing every possible subset of the instances X.

Hence, represent the hypothesis as a disjunction of hypotheses rather than converting an attribute to '?'.

For example,

<Sunny, ?, ?, ?, ?, ?>∨<Cloudy, ?, ?, ?, ?, ?>

This ensures allowing only sunny or cloudy as the value for 'Yes' outcome.

18. What is machine learning? Explain different perspectives and issues in machine learning. (6M) (SEP 2020)

Definition: Machine Learning

Machine learning is a field where a computer program is said to learn from experience E with respect to some class of tasks T and performance measure P, if its performance at tasks in T, as measured by P, improves with experience E.

Perspectives and issues in machine learning

Perspective

- Machine learning involves searching a very large space of possible hypotheses to determine one that best fits the observed data and any prior knowledge held by the learner.
- The LMS algorithm for fitting weights achieves this goal by iteratively tuning the weights, adding a correction to each weight each time the hypothesized evaluation function predicts a value that differs from the training value.

Issues in Machine Learning

The field of machine learning, and much of this book, is concerned with answering questions such as the following

- What algorithms exist for learning general target functions from specific training examples? In what settings will particular algorithms converge to the desired function, given sufficient training data? Which algorithms perform best for which types of problems and representations?
- How much training data is sufficient? What general bounds can be found to relate the confidence in learned hypotheses to the amount of training experience and the character of the learner's hypothesis space?
- When and how can prior knowledge held by the learner guide the process of generalizing from examples? Can prior knowledge be helpful even when it is only approximately correct?
- What is the best strategy for choosing a useful next training experience, and how does the choice of this strategy alter the complexity of the learning problem?
- What is the best way to reduce the learning task to one or more function approximation problems? Put another way, what specific functions should the system attempt to learn? Can this process itself be automated?
- How can the learner automatically alter its representation to improve its ability to represent and learn the target function?

19. Explain the steps in designing the learning system. (10M) (SEP 2020)

REFER QUESTION - 2

20. Describe the Candidate Elimination algorithm. Explain its working, taking the enjoy sport concept and training instances given below.

Sl. No.	Sky	AirTemp	Humidity	Wind	Water	Forecast	EnjoySport
1	Sunny	Warm	Normal	Strong	Warm	Same	Yes
2	Sunny	Warm	High	Strong	Warm	Same	Yes
3	Rainy	Cool	High	Strong	Warm	Change	No
4	Sunny	Warm	High	Strong	Warm	Change	Yes

(6M) (SEP 2020)

REFER QP PROBLEM SOLUTIONS

MODULE 2

DECISION TREE LEARNING

1. **What is decision tree? Discuss the use of decision tree for classification purpose with an example. (8M) (JAN 19)**

Decision tree learning is a method for approximating discrete-valued target functions, in which the learned function is represented by a decision tree.

Decision Tree classification

- Decision trees classify instances by sorting them down the tree from the root to some leaf node, which provides the classification of the instance.
- Each node in the tree specifies a test of some attribute of the instance, and each branch descending from that node corresponds to one of the possible values for this attribute.
- An instance is classified by starting at the root node of the tree, testing the attribute specified by this node, then moving down the tree branch corresponding to the value of the attribute in the given example. This process is then repeated for the subtree rooted at the new node.

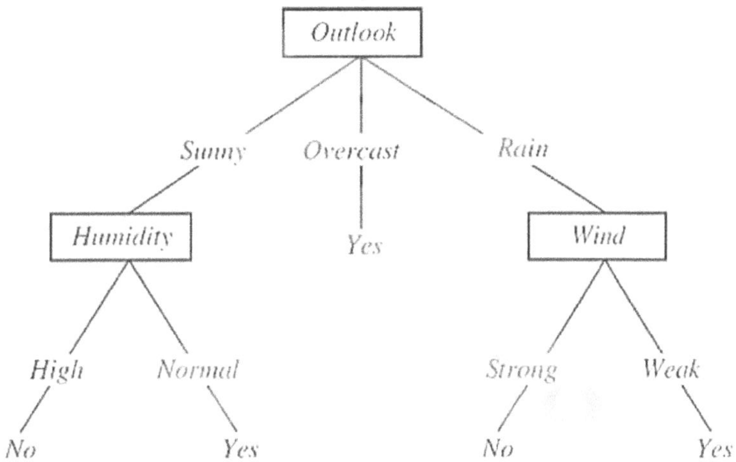

FIGURE: A decision tree for the concept ***PlayTennis***. An example is classified by sorting it through the tree to the appropriate leaf node, then returning the classification associated with this leaf

- Decision trees represent a disjunction of conjunctions of constraints on the attribute values of instances.
- Each path from the tree root to a leaf corresponds to a conjunction of attribute tests, and the tree itself to a disjunction of these conjunctions

For example, the decision tree shown in above figure corresponds to the expression (Outlook = Sunny ∧ Humidity = Normal) ∨ (Outlook = Overcast) (Outlook = Rain ∧ Wind = Weak)

2. **Write and explain the decision tree for the following transactions.**

Tid	Refund	MaritalStatus	TaxableIncome	Cheat
1	Yes	Single	125k	No
2	No	Married	100k	No
3	No	Single	70k	No
4	Yes	Married	120k	No
5	No	Divorced	95k	Yes
6	No	Married	60k	No
7	Yes	Divorced	220k	No
8	No	Single	85k	Yes
9	No	Married	75k	No
10	No	Single	90k	Yes

(8M) (JAN 19)

Attributes

Refund $\rightarrow$ {Yes, No}

MaritalStatus $\rightarrow$ {Single, Married, Divorced}

TaxableIncome $\rightarrow$ {continuous-valued}

Refer Old QP Problem Solutions

3. **For the transactions shown in the table, compute the following:**
   a. **Entropy of the collection of transaction records of the table with respect to classification**
   b. **What are the information gain of a_1 and a_2 relative to the transaction of the table?**

Instance	1	2	3	4	5	6	7	8	9
a_1	T	T	T	F	F	F	F	T	F
a_2	T	T	F	F	T	T	F	F	T
TargetClass	+	+	-	+	-	-	-	+	-

(8M) (JAN 19)

Refer Old QP Problem Solutions

4. **Discuss the decision learning algorithm. (4M) (JAN 19)** ID3(Examples, Target_attribute, Attributes)

Examples are the training examples. Target_attribute is the attribute whose value is to be predicted by the tree. Attributes is a list of other attributes that may be tested by the learned decision tree. Returns a decision tree that correctly classifies the given Examples.

- Create a Root node for the tree
- If all Examples are positive, Return the single-node tree Root, with label = +
- If all Examples are negative, Return the single-node tree Root, with label = -
- If Attributes is empty, Return the single-node tree Root, with label = most common value of Target_attribute in Examples
- Otherwise Begin
  - A ← the attribute from Attributes that best* classifies Examples
  - The decision attribute for Root ← A

- For each possible value, *vi*, of A,
  - Add a new tree branch below *Root*, corresponding to the test A =
  - *vi* Let *Examples vi*, be the subset of Examples that have value *vi*
  - for *A* If *Examples vi* , is empty
    - Then below this new branch add a leaf node with label = most common value of Target_attribute in Examples
    - Else below this new branch add the subtree
      ID3(*Examples vi*, Targe_tattribute, Attributes – {A}))

- End
- Return Root

The best attribute is the one with highest information gain. ID3 is a greedy algorithm that grows the tree top-down, at each node selecting the attribute that best classifies the local training examples. This process continues until the tree perfectly classifies the training examples, or until all attributes have been used.

- The central choice in the ID3 algorithm is selecting which attribute to test at each node in the tree.
- A statistical property called ***information gain*** that measures how well a given attribute separates the training examples according to their target classification.
- ID3 uses ***information gain*** measure to select among the candidate attributes at each step while growing the tree.

To define information gain, we begin by defining a measure called entropy. *Entropy measures the impurity of a collection of examples.*

Given a collection S, containing positive and negative examples of some target concept, the entropy of S relative to this Boolean classification is

$$Entropy(S) \equiv -p_{\oplus} \log_2 p_{\oplus} - p_{\ominus} \log_2 p_{\ominus}$$

Where,

$p+$ is the proportion of positive examples in S

$p-$ is the proportion of negative examples in S.

5. List the issues of decision tree learning. (4M) (JAN 19)

Avoiding overfitting the data

Reduced-Error Pruning

- Reduced-error pruning, is to consider each of the decision nodes in the tree to be candidates for pruning
- ***Pruning*** a decision node consists of removing the subtree rooted at that node, making it a leaf node, and assigning it the most common classification of the training examples affiliated with that node
- Nodes are removed only if the resulting pruned tree performs no worse than-the original over the validation set.

Reduced error pruning has the effect that any leaf node added due to coincidental regularities in the training set is likely to be pruned because these same coincidences are unlikely to occur in the validation set

Rule Post-Pruning

- Rule post-pruning involves the following steps:
- Infer the decision tree from the training set, growing the tree until the training data is fit as well as possible and allowing overfitting to occur.
- Convert the learned tree into an equivalent set of rules by creating one rule for each path from the root node to a leaf node.
- Prune(generalize) each rule by removing any preconditions that result in improving its estimated accuracy.

Sort the pruned rules by their estimated accuracy, and consider them in this sequence when classifying subsequent instances.

Incorporating Continuous-Valued Attributes

i. Define new discrete valued attributes that partition the continuous attribute value into a discrete set of intervals.
   E.g., {high ≡ Temp > 35° C, med ≡ 10° C < Temp ≤ 35° C, low ≡ Temp ≤ 10° C}

ii. Using thresholds for splitting nodes
e.g., A ≤ a produces subsets A ≤ a and A > a

Alternative Measures for Selecting Attributes

- The problem is if attributes with many values, Gain will select it ?
- Example: consider the attribute Date, which has a very large number of possible values. (e.g., March 4, 1979).
- If this attribute is added to the PlayTennis data, it would have the highest information gain of any of the attributes. This is because Date alone perfectly predicts the target attribute over the training data. Thus, it would be selected as the decision attribute for the root node of the tree and lead to a tree of depth one, which perfectly classifies the training data.
- This decision tree with root node Date is not a useful predictor because it perfectly separates the training data, but poorly predict on subsequent examples.

Handling Training Examples with Missing Attribute Values

- If node n test A, assign most common value of A among other training examples sorted to node n
- Assign most common value of A among other training examples with same target value
- Assign a probability pi to each of the possible values vi of A rather than simply assigning the most common value to A(x)

Handling Attributes with Differing Costs

- In some learning tasks the instance attributes may have associated costs.
- For example: In learning to classify medical diseases, the patients described in terms of attributes such as Temperature, BiopsyResult, Pulse, BloodTestResults, etc.
    - These attributes vary significantly in their costs, both in terms of monetary cost and cost to patient comfort
    - Decision trees use low-cost attributes where possible, depends only on high-cost attributes only when needed to produce reliable classifications

6. Construct the decision tree for the following data using ID3 algorithm.

Day	A1	A2	A3	Classification
1	True	Hot	High	No
2	True	Hot	High	No
3	False	Hot	High	Yes
4	False	Cool	Normal	Yes
5	False	Cool	Normal	Yes
6	True	Cool	High	No
7	True	Hot	High	No
8	True	Hot	Normal	Yes
9	False	Cool	Normal	Yes
10	False	Cool	High	No

(16M)(JULY 19)

Refer Old QP Problem Solutions

7. Explain the concept of decision tree learning. Discuss the necessary measures required to select the attributes for building a decision tree using ID3 algorithm. (8M)JULY 19)

Refer Question - 4

8. Discuss the issues of avoiding overfitting the data, handling continuous data and missing values in decision tree. (8M)(JULY 19)

Refer Question – 5

9. Discuss the two approaches to prevent over fitting the data. (8M) (JAN 2020)

10. Consider the following set of training examples:

instance	Classification	a_1	a_2
1	1	1	1
2	1	1	1
3	0	1	0
4	1	0	0
5	0	0	1
6	0	0	1

i. **What is the entropy of this collection of training examples with respect to the target function classification?**

ii. **What is the information gain of a_2 relative to these training examples?**

(8M) (JAN 2020)

Refer Old QP Problem Solutions

11. Define decision tree. Construct the decision tree to represent the following Boolean functions:

i) A∧¬B   ii) A∨[B∧C]   iii) A XOR B

(6M) (JAN 2020)

Refer Old QP Problem Solutions

https://youtu.be/CSa6x4uP0Ms

12. Write the ID3 algorithm. (6M) (JAN 2020)

Refer Question - 4

13. What do you mean by gain and entropy? How is it used to build the decision tree? (4M) (JAN 2020)

Entropy *measures the impurity of a collection of examples.*

Given a collection S, containing positive and negative examples of some target concept, the entropy of S relative to this Boolean classification is

$$\text{Entropy}(S) \equiv \quad p_{\oplus} \log_2 p_{\oplus} \quad p_{-} \log_2 p_{-}$$

Where,

$p_{\oplus} \rightarrow$ proportion of positive examples in S

$p \rightarrow$ proportion of negative examples in S.

Information Gain, is the expected reduction in entropy caused by partitioning the examples according to this attribute.

The information gain, Gain(S, A) of an attribute A, relative to a collection of examples S, is defined as

$$Gain(S, A) = Entropy(S) - {}_{v\ Values(A)} \frac{|S_v|}{|S|} Entropy(S_v)$$

To select a root node/a node, apply Entropy for each attribute and use it to compute the Information Gain of these attributes. The attribute with the **highest information gain** is set as the root node or the next node in the sub tree.

14. Explain the concept of entropy and information gain. (6M) (SEP 2020)

Refer Question – 13

15. Describe the ID3 algorithm for decision tree learning. (10M) (SEP 2020)

Refer Question – 4

16. Apply ID3 algorithm for constructing decision tree for the following training example. (10M) (SEP 2020)

Day	Outlook	Temperature	Humidity	Wind	PlayTennis
D1	Sunny	Hot	High	Weak	No
D2	Sunny	Hot	High	Strong	No
D3	Overcast	Hot	High	Weak	Yes
D4	Rain	Mild	High	Weak	Yes
D5	Rain	Cool	Normal	Weak	Yes
D6	Rain	Cool	Normal	Strong	No
D7	Overcast	Cool	Normal	Strong	Yes
D8	Sunny	Mild	High	Weak	No
D9	Sunny	Cool	Normal	Weak	Yes
D10	Rain	Mild	Normal	Weak	Yes
D11	Sunny	Mild	Normal	Strong	Yes
D12	Overcast	Mild	High	Strong	Yes
D13	Overcast	Hot	Normal	Weak	Yes
D14	Rain	Mild	High	strong	No

(10M) (SEP 2020)

Refer Old QP Problem Solutions

17. Explain the issues in decision tree learning. (6M) (SEP 2020)

Refer Question – 5

MODULE 3

ARTIFICIAL NEURAL NETWORKS

Rewritten with clear explanations and complete, runnable Python examples. Topics follow the typical VTU Module-3 syllabus: Perceptron, Gradient Descent / Delta Rule, Multi-layer networks, Back-propagation, and practical applications.

1. The Perceptron

A perceptron is the simplest neural network unit. It takes a vector of real-valued inputs, computes a weighted sum, and applies a threshold (step) activation to produce a binary output.

Decision rule: $o = 1$ if $w \cdot x + b > 0$, else $o = 0$ (or -1 in the bipolar version).

Geometrically the weight vector defines a hyperplane that separates the two classes. The classic perceptron learning algorithm is guaranteed to find a separating hyperplane when the data are linearly separable.

Python – Perceptron from scratch (NumPy)

```
import numpy as np

class Perceptron:
    def __init__(self, n_features, lr=0.1, n_epochs=50):
        self.w = np.zeros(n_features)
        self.b = 0.0
        self.lr = lr
        self.n_epochs = n_epochs

    def predict(self, X):
        return np.where(X @ self.w + self.b >= 0, 1, 0)

    def fit(self, X, y):
        for _ in range(self.n_epochs):
            for xi, yi in zip(X, y):
                update = self.lr * (yi - self.predict(xi.reshape(1, -1))[0])
                self.w += update * xi
                self.b += update
        return self

# AND gate example
X = np.array([[0,0],[0,1],[1,0],[1,1]], dtype=float)
y = np.array([0, 0, 0, 1])           # AND
clf = Perceptron(n_features=2).fit(X, y)
print("Weights:", clf.w, "Bias:", clf.b)
print("Predictions:", clf.predict(X))
```

The same class works for OR and for any linearly separable binary classification problem. For XOR the algorithm will never converge — that is the classic motivation for multi-layer networks.

2. Gradient Descent and the Delta Rule

When we replace the hard threshold by a differentiable activation (usually the sigmoid or tanh), we can minimise a continuous error function by gradient descent. The resulting weight update is known as the **delta rule** (or LMS rule):

$\Delta w_i = \eta (t - o) x_i$ where t is the target and o is the network output.

For a sigmoid unit the derivative $\sigma'(net) = \sigma(net)(1-\sigma(net))$ appears, giving the well-known logistic-regression update.

Python – Delta rule / logistic unit

```
import numpy as np

def sigmoid(z):
    return 1 / (1 + np.exp(-np.clip(z, -40, 40)))
```

```
class DeltaRule:
    def __init__(self, n_features, lr=0.5, n_epochs=2000):
        self.w = np.random.randn(n_features) * 0.1
        self.b = 0.0
        self.lr = lr
        self.n_epochs = n_epochs

    def predict_proba(self, X):
        return sigmoid(X @ self.w + self.b)

    def fit(self, X, y):
        for _ in range(self.n_epochs):
            o = self.predict_proba(X)
            error = y - o
            # gradient of MSE (or cross-entropy up to a constant)
            self.w += self.lr * (X.T @ (error * o * (1 - o))) / len(y)
            self.b += self.lr * np.mean(error * o * (1 - o))
        return self

# Learning a soft OR
X = np.array([[0,0],[0,1],[1,0],[1,1]], dtype=float)
y = np.array([0., 1., 1., 1.])
model = DeltaRule(2).fit(X, y)
print(np.round(model.predict_proba(X), 3))
```

3. Multi-layer Feed-forward Networks

A multi-layer perceptron (MLP) stacks several layers of sigmoid (or ReLU) units. The hidden layers allow the network to form non-linear decision surfaces and therefore to solve problems such as XOR that a single perceptron cannot.

Universal approximation theorem (Hornik et al.): a feed-forward network with a single hidden layer containing a sufficient number of non-linear units can approximate any continuous function on a compact set to arbitrary accuracy.

Python – XOR solved by a 2-2-1 network

```
import numpy as np

def sigmoid(z):
    return 1 / (1 + np.exp(-np.clip(z, -40, 40)))
def sigmoid_prime(a):
    return a * (1 - a)

X = np.array([[0,0],[0,1],[1,0],[1,1]], dtype=float)
y = np.array([[0],[1],[1],[0]], dtype=float)    # XOR

np.random.seed(1)
W1 = np.random.randn(2, 2) * 0.5    # input -> hidden
b1 = np.zeros((1, 2))
W2 = np.random.randn(2, 1) * 0.5    # hidden -> output
b2 = np.zeros((1, 1))

lr = 0.7
for epoch in range(8000):
    # forward
    a1 = sigmoid(X @ W1 + b1)
    a2 = sigmoid(a1 @ W2 + b2)
    # backward
    dz2 = (a2 - y) * sigmoid_prime(a2)
    dW2 = a1.T @ dz2
    db2 = np.sum(dz2, axis=0, keepdims=True)
    dz1 = (dz2 @ W2.T) * sigmoid_prime(a1)
    dW1 = X.T @ dz1
    db1 = np.sum(dz1, axis=0, keepdims=True)
    # update
    W2 -= lr * dW2;  b2 -= lr * db2
    W1 -= lr * dW1;  b1 -= lr * db1

print("XOR predictions:", np.round(a2.ravel(), 3))
```

4. Back-propagation Algorithm

Back-propagation is simply the efficient application of the chain rule to compute the gradient of the loss with respect to every weight in a multi-layer network. The algorithm consists of a forward pass that computes all activations, followed by a backward pass that propagates error derivatives from the output layer back to the input.

Key steps:

1. Forward-propagate the input to obtain the output o.
2. Compute the output-layer error term $\delta_k = (t_k - o_k)\, o_k\, (1 - o_k)$.
3. For each hidden unit h compute $\delta_h = o_h(1 - o_h)\, \Sigma_k\, w_{kh}\, \delta_k$.
4. Update every weight: $\Delta w_{ji} = \eta\, \delta_j\, x_{ji}$.

Python – Generic back-prop trainer (one hidden layer)

```
import numpy as np

class MLP:
    def __init__(self, n_in, n_hidden, n_out, lr=0.5):
        self.W1 = np.random.randn(n_in, n_hidden) * 0.5
        self.b1 = np.zeros((1, n_hidden))
        self.W2 = np.random.randn(n_hidden, n_out) * 0.5
        self.b2 = np.zeros((1, n_out))
        self.lr = lr

    def _sigmoid(self, z):
        return 1 / (1 + np.exp(-np.clip(z, -40, 40)))

    def forward(self, X):
        self.a1 = self._sigmoid(X @ self.W1 + self.b1)
        self.a2 = self._sigmoid(self.a1 @ self.W2 + self.b2)
        return self.a2

    def backward(self, X, y):
        m = len(y)
        dz2 = (self.a2 - y) * self.a2 * (1 - self.a2)
        dW2 = self.a1.T @ dz2 / m
        db2 = np.mean(dz2, axis=0, keepdims=True)
        dz1 = (dz2 @ self.W2.T) * self.a1 * (1 - self.a1)
        dW1 = X.T @ dz1 / m
        db1 = np.mean(dz1, axis=0, keepdims=True)
        self.W2 -= self.lr * dW2; self.b2 -= self.lr * db2
        self.W1 -= self.lr * dW1; self.b1 -= self.lr * db1

    def fit(self, X, y, epochs=5000):
        for _ in range(epochs):
            self.forward(X)
            self.backward(X, y)
        return self

# Example: learn a simple non-linear function
X = np.random.randn(200, 2)
y = (X[:,0]**2 + X[:,1]**2 < 1).astype(float).reshape(-1,1)  # inside unit circle
net = MLP(2, 8, 1, lr=0.8).fit(X, y, epochs=3000)
acc = np.mean((net.forward(X) > 0.5) == y)
print(f"Training accuracy: {acc:.3f}")
```

5. Practical Issues & Applications

Over-fitting – Neural nets can memorise noise. Common remedies: early stopping, weight decay (L2 regularisation), dropout, and simply using more training data.

Local minima – Gradient descent can become stuck. In practice random restarts, momentum, or modern optimisers (Adam) largely mitigate the problem.

Classic application (ALVINN) – A 30×32 retina of pixel intensities was fed to a back-propagation network that output a steering direction. The system successfully drove a vehicle at highway speeds, demonstrating that multi-layer nets can learn complex sensorimotor mappings from real data.

Python – Quick regularised training sketch

```
# L2 weight decay added to the weight update (inside the training loop):
# self.W2 -= self.lr * (dW2 + lambd * self.W2)
# self.W1 -= self.lr * (dW1 + lambd * self.W1)
# Typical values: lambd = 1e-4 ... 1e-3
print("Add weight-decay term to any of the trainers above to reduce over-fitting.")
```

6. Selected VTU-style Questions Answered with Code

Q1. Derive the gradient-descent weight update for a single sigmoid unit and implement it.

See the DeltaRule class above. The derivation follows from $\partial E/\partial w_i = -(t-o)\sigma'(net)x_i$ and the update $w \leftarrow w - \eta\, \partial E/\partial w$.

Q2. Show that a single perceptron cannot realise XOR. Demonstrate a two-layer network that can.

A perceptron implements a linear threshold function; XOR is not linearly separable. The 2-2-1 network in Section 3 converges to the correct XOR mapping.

Q3. Write a Python program for the back-propagation algorithm and test it on a small data set.

The MLP class in Section 4 is a complete, self-contained implementation. It can be tested on any numeric data set of compatible shape.

— End of rewritten Module 3 — All code blocks are self-contained and run with only NumPy.

MODULE 4

BAYESIAN LEARNING

Completely rewritten with clear theory, diagrams, and runnable Python examples. Covers Bayes' theorem, MAP & ML hypotheses, Naïve Bayes classifier, Bayesian networks, and the Minimum Description Length principle.

1. Bayes' Theorem

Bayes' theorem tells us how to update our belief in a hypothesis h after observing data D:

P(h|D) = P(D|h) P(h) / P(D)

- **P(h)** – prior probability of the hypothesis (before seeing data)
- **P(D|h)** – likelihood of the data given the hypothesis
- **P(D)** – marginal probability of the data (normalising constant)
- **P(h|D)** – posterior probability (after seeing the data)

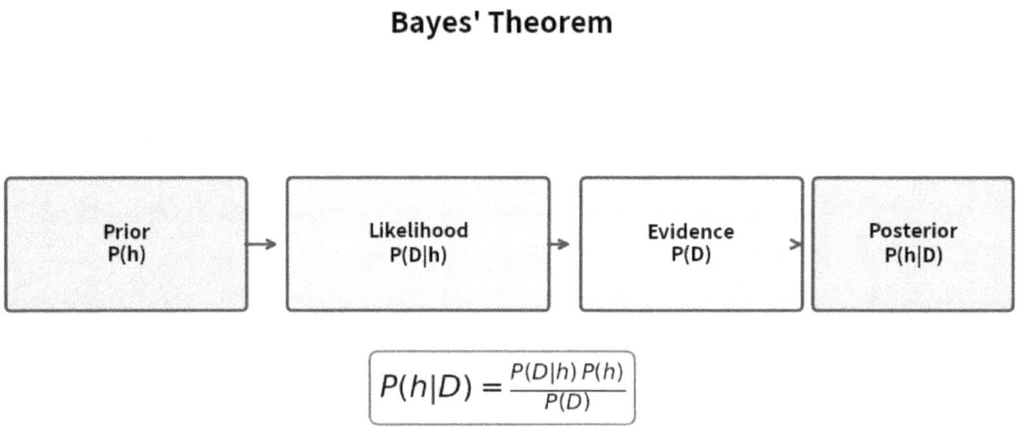

2. Maximum a Posteriori (MAP) and Maximum Likelihood (ML)

In learning we usually want the single best hypothesis. Two common choices are:

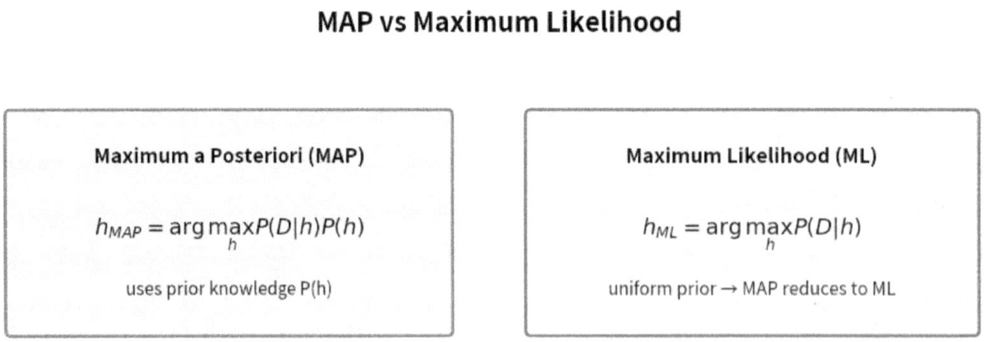

When every hypothesis is considered equally likely a priori, MAP reduces to ML. Many classical learning algorithms (linear regression under Gaussian noise, etc.) can be derived as maximum-likelihood estimators.

Python – Computing MAP for a tiny hypothesis space

```
import numpy as np

# Hypotheses: three possible biases of a coin
# h1: P(H)=0.3 , h2: P(H)=0.5 , h3: P(H)=0.8
hyps = {'h1': 0.3, 'h2': 0.5, 'h3': 0.8}
```

```
prior = {'H1': 0.2, 'H2': 0.5, 'H3': 0.3}    # prior beliefs

# Observed data: 3 Heads, 1 Tail
data = ['H', 'H', 'H', 'T']

def likelihood(theta, data):
    return np.prod([theta if d=='H' else 1-theta for d in data])

# Posterior (un-normalised) then normalise
post = {}
for h, theta in hyps.items():
    post[h] = likelihood(theta, data) * prior[h]
Z = sum(post.values())
post = {h: v/Z for h, v in post.items()}

print("Posteriors:", {h: round(p, 3) for h, p in post.items()})
print("MAP hypothesis:", max(post, key=post.get))
```

3. Naïve Bayes Classifier

Naïve Bayes assumes that the attributes are **conditionally independent** given the class label. This dramatically simplifies the computation of the posterior:

$P(y \mid a1 \ldots an) \propto P(y) \prod_i P(ai \mid y)$

Despite the strong independence assumption, Naïve Bayes often works surprisingly well in practice (text classification, spam filtering, medical diagnosis, etc.).

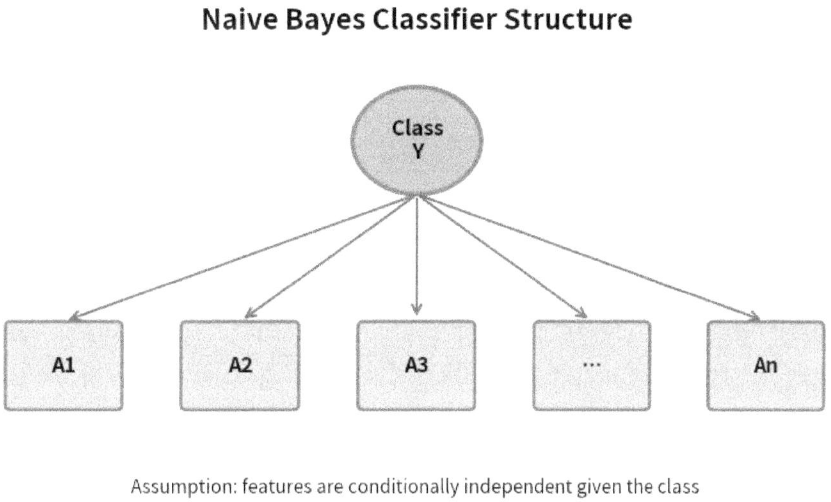

Python – Complete Naïve Bayes (Laplace-smoothed) on the classic Play-Tennis data

```
from collections import defaultdict
import math

data = [  # outlook, temp, humidity, wind, play
    ("Sunny","Hot","High","Weak","No"), ("Sunny","Hot","High","Strong","No"),
    ("Overcast","Hot","High","Weak","Yes"), ("Rain","Mild","High","Weak","Yes"),
    ("Rain","Cool","Normal","Weak","Yes"), ("Rain","Cool","Normal","Strong","No"),
    ("Overcast","Cool","Normal","Strong","Yes"), ("Sunny","Mild","High","Weak","No"),
    ("Sunny","Cool","Normal","Weak","Yes"), ("Rain","Mild","Normal","Weak","Yes"),
    ("Sunny","Mild","Normal","Strong","Yes"), ("Overcast","Mild","High","Strong","Yes"),
    ("Overcast","Hot","Normal","Weak","Yes"), ("Rain","Mild","High","Strong","No"),
]

def train(data, alpha=1.0):
    class_cnt = defaultdict(int)
    feat_cnt  = defaultdict(lambda: defaultdict(lambda: defaultdict(int)))
    for *xs, y in data:
        class_cnt[y] += 1
        for i, v in enumerate(xs):
            feat_cnt[i][v][y] += 1
    return class_cnt, feat_cnt

def predict(class_cnt, feat_cnt, x, alpha=1.0, n_vals=(3,3,2,2)):
    total = sum(class_cnt.values())
```

```
    scores = {}
    for c, cnt in class_cnt.items():
        logp = math.log((cnt + alpha) / (total + alpha * len(class_cnt)))
        for i, v in enumerate(x):
            logp += math.log((feat_cnt[i][v][c] + alpha) / (cnt + alpha * n_vals[i]))
        scores[c] = logp
    return max(scores, key=scores.get), scores

cc, fc = train(data)
label, scores = predict(cc, fc, ("Sunny", "Cool", "High", "Strong"))
print("Predicted:", label)
print("Log-scores:", {k: round(v, 3) for k, v in scores.items()})
```

4. Bayesian Networks

A Bayesian network is a directed acyclic graph (DAG) whose nodes are random variables and whose edges encode conditional dependencies. Each node stores a conditional probability table (CPT) given its parents. The joint distribution factorises as:

$P(X1...Xn) = \Pi_i P(Xi \mid Parents(Xi))$

Example Bayesian Network (Alarm)

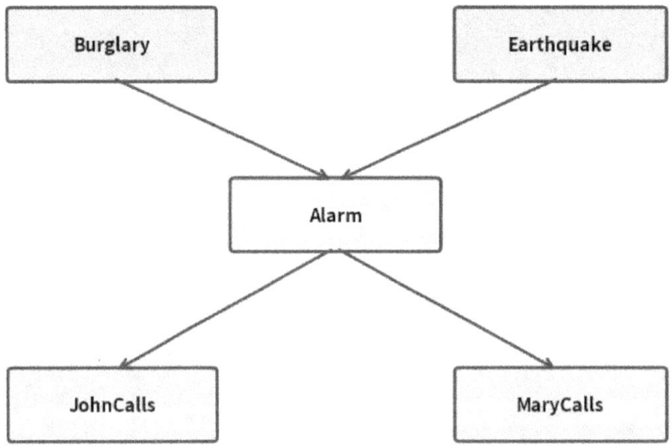

The classic "Alarm" network (Pearl) shows how a burglary or an earthquake can trigger an alarm, which in turn causes John and Mary to call. Exact inference can be performed by variable elimination or belief propagation; for larger nets we resort to approximate methods (MCMC, variational).

Python – Tiny Bayesian-network inference (enumeration)

```
# Extremely small BN:  Burglary -> Alarm <- Earthquake
# We compute P(Burglary | JohnCalls=True) by enumeration

# CPTs (hard-coded)
P_B = 0.001
P_E = 0.002
# P(A | B, E)
P_A = {(True,True):0.95, (True,False):0.94, (False,True):0.29, (False,False):0.001}
# P(J | A)
P_J = {True:0.90, False:0.05}

def joint(b, e, a, j):
    return (P_B if b else 1-P_B) * (P_E if e else 1-P_E) * P_A[(b,e)] * (P_J[a] if j else 1-P_J[a])

# P(B=True | J=True)  =  sum_{e,a} P(B=T,e,a,J=T)  /  sum_{b,e,a} P(b,e,a,J=T)
num = sum(joint(True, e, a, True) for e in [True,False] for a in [True,False])
den = sum(joint(b, e, a, True) for b in [True,False] for e in [True,False] for a in [True,False])
print(f"P(Burglary | JohnCalls) ≈ {num/den:.4f}")
```

5. Minimum Description Length (MDL) Principle

Occam's razor formalised in information-theoretic terms: choose the hypothesis that minimises the total number of bits needed to encode the hypothesis plus the data given the hypothesis:

$h_{MDL} = \arg\min_h (L_{C1}(h) + L_{C2}(D|h))$

where $L_C(\cdot)$ denotes description length under an optimal code. Under a suitable choice of codes this is equivalent to the MAP hypothesis. MDL automatically balances model complexity against data fit and is therefore a principled way to avoid over-fitting.

6. Selected VTU-style Questions (answered)

Q1. State Bayes' theorem and explain each term. (4 M)

See Section 1 and the accompanying diagram.

Q2. Distinguish MAP and ML hypotheses. When do they coincide? (6 M)

See Section 2. They coincide when the prior is uniform.

Q3. Explain the Naïve Bayes classifier and give a worked example. (8 M)

Section 3 contains the full derivation, a structural diagram, and a complete Python implementation on the Play-Tennis data set.

Q4. What is a Bayesian network? Illustrate with an example. (8 M)

Section 4 + the Alarm network diagram + a minimal inference program.

— End of rewritten Module 4 — All programs run with pure Python / NumPy only.

MODULE 5

EVALUATING HYPOTHESES · INSTANCE-BASED LEARNING · REINFORCEMENT LEARNING

Fully rewritten with diagrams and runnable Python. Covers hypothesis accuracy & confidence intervals, k-Nearest Neighbours, and Q-learning with a grid-world demo.

1. Evaluating Hypothesis Accuracy

After learning a hypothesis *h* we need an estimate of its true error on the whole instance space. We draw a test sample of size *n* and count the number of mistakes *r*. The observed error is **$error_S(h) = r/n$**.

Under the binomial model the number of errors follows Binomial(*n*, $error_D(h)$). A normal approximation yields a confidence interval:

$error_D(h) \in error_S(h) \pm z_c \sqrt{(error_S(1-error_S)/n)}$

where z_c = 1.96 for a 95 % interval (large *n*).

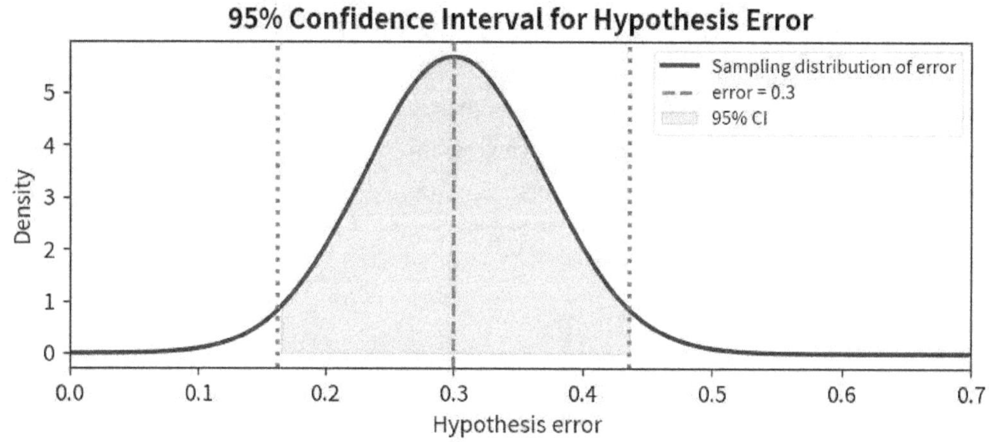

Python – Confidence interval for hypothesis error

```
import math

def confidence_interval(r, n, z=1.96):
    """r = number of errors, n = test-set size"""
    p = r / n
    se = math.sqrt(p * (1 - p) / n)
    return p - z * se, p + z * se

# Example: 12 errors on 100 test examples
lo, hi = confidence_interval(12, 100)
print(f"Observed error = 0.12")
print(f"95% CI ≈ [{lo:.3f}, {hi:.3f}]")
```

2. Instance-Based Learning – k-Nearest Neighbours

Instance-based methods store the training examples and delay generalisation until a query arrives. The most popular algorithm is **k-Nearest Neighbours (k-NN)**:

1. Given query x_q, find the k training instances closest to x_q (usually Euclidean distance).
2. For classification return the majority class among those k neighbours.
3. For regression return the average of the k target values.

1-NN produces a Voronoi tessellation of the instance space; larger k yields smoother decision boundaries but can also smooth away genuine structure.

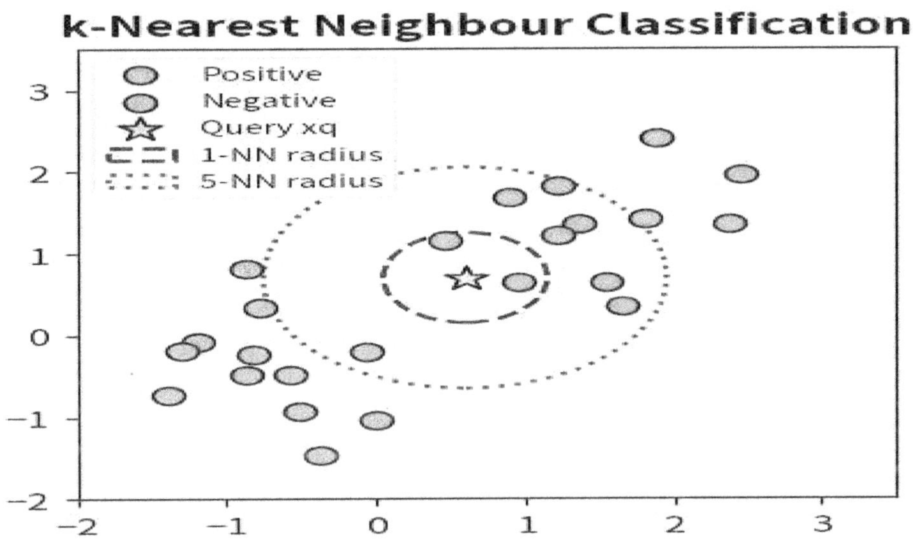

Python – k-NN classifier from scratch

```
import numpy as np
from collections import Counter

class KNN:
    def __init__(self, k=3):
        self.k = k
    def fit(self, X, y):
        self.X, self.y = np.asarray(X, float), np.asarray(y)
        return self
    def predict(self, Xq):
        Xq = np.atleast_2d(Xq)
        preds = []
        for q in Xq:
            dists = np.linalg.norm(self.X - q, axis=1)
            idx = np.argsort(dists)[:self.k]
            preds.append(Counter(self.y[idx]).most_common(1)[0][0])
        return np.array(preds)

# Tiny demo
X = [[1,2],[2,3],[3,1],[6,5],[7,7],[8,6]]
y = [0,0,0,1,1,1]
clf = KNN(k=3).fit(X, y)
print("Prediction for [4,4]:", clf.predict([[4,4]])[0])
print("Prediction for [7,5]:", clf.predict([[7,5]])[0])
```

3. Reinforcement Learning & Q-Learning

In reinforcement learning an agent interacts with an environment by taking actions and receiving rewards. The goal is to learn a policy that maximises expected cumulative reward.

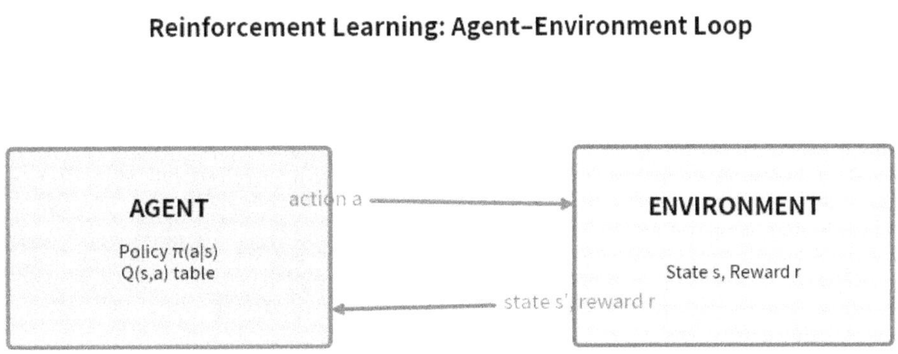

Q-learning is a model-free off-policy algorithm that learns the action-value function Q(s,a). The update rule is:

$Q(s,a) \leftarrow Q(s,a) + \alpha\,[\,r + \gamma \max_{a'} Q(s',a') - Q(s,a)\,]$

where α is the learning rate and γ the discount factor. Under standard conditions Q-learning converges to the optimal Q^* for any exploration policy that visits every state-action pair infinitely often.

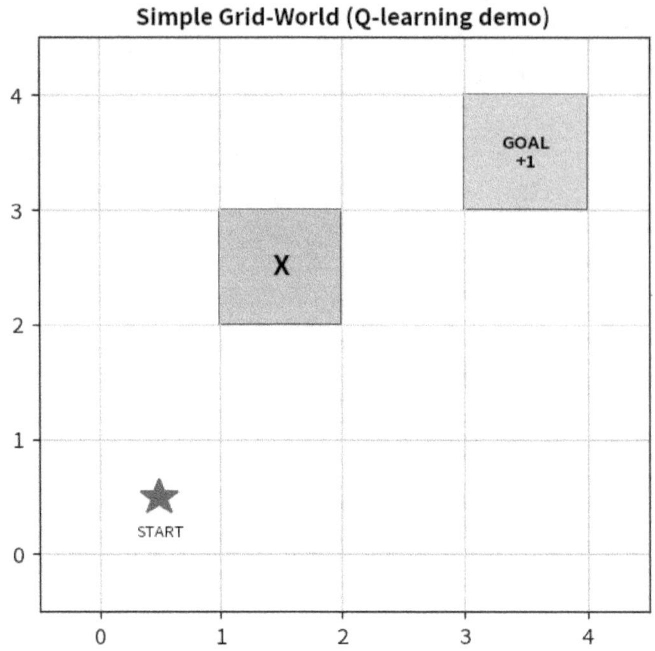

Python – Q-learning on a tiny grid-world

```
import numpy as np

# 4x4 grid, goal at (3,3), obstacle at (1,2)
n = 4
actions = [(0,1),(0,-1),(1,0),(-1,0)]  # N S E W
Q = np.zeros((n, n, 4))
alpha, gamma, eps = 0.3, 0.9, 0.2
goal = (3, 3)
obstacle = (1, 2)

def step(s, a):
    ns = (s[0] + actions[a][0], s[1] + actions[a][1])
    if not (0 <= ns[0] < n and 0 <= ns[1] < n) or ns == obstacle:
        return s, -0.1          # bump into wall / obstacle
    if ns == goal:
        return ns, +1.0
    return ns, -0.01

for episode in range(800):
    s = (0, 0)
    while s != goal:
        if np.random.rand() < eps:
            a = np.random.randint(4)
        else:
            a = np.argmax(Q[s[0], s[1]])
        ns, r = step(s, a)
        Q[s[0], s[1], a] += alpha * (r + gamma * np.max(Q[ns[0], ns[1]]) - Q[s[0], s[1], a])
        s = ns

# Greedy policy from start
s = (0, 0)
path = [s]
for _ in range(20):
    if s == goal: break
    a = np.argmax(Q[s[0], s[1]])
    s, _ = step(s, a)
    path.append(s)
print("Learned path:", path)
print("Q-values at start:", np.round(Q[0,0], 2))
```

4. Selected VTU-style Questions (answered)

Q1. How do you estimate the accuracy of a hypothesis? Derive a confidence interval. (8 M)

Section 1 + the binomial / normal-approximation formula and the Python helper.

Q2. Explain the k-Nearest Neighbour algorithm with a diagram. (6 M)

Section 2 contains the algorithm, a visual illustration, and a complete implementation.

Q3. Write the Q-learning update rule and illustrate with a simple example. (8 M)

Section 3 gives the update, the agent–environment diagram, a grid-world figure, and a full Q-learning program that learns a path to the goal.

— End of rewritten Module 5 — All code runs with pure Python / NumPy.

Appendix: Python Examples for Core AI Topics

These short, self-contained examples illustrate key ideas from the notes: propositional/predicate-style reasoning, Bayesian inference, a simple neural network, and basic logic operations. They are intended for quick experimentation.

1. Simple Logic Reasoning (Propositional)

Resolution-style checking of a small knowledge base. We represent clauses as sets of literals and perform a basic resolution step.

```
# Simple propositional resolution example
# Knowledge base (clauses as frozensets of literals)
# ~P v Q ,  P ,  ~Q v R   |=  R ?

kb = [
    frozenset(["~P", "Q"]),
    frozenset(["P"]),
    frozenset(["~Q", "R"]),
]

def resolve(c1, c2):
    """Return resolvents of two clauses (if any)."""
    resolvents = []
    for lit in c1:
        neg = lit[1:] if lit.startswith("~") else "~" + lit
        if neg in c2:
            new = (c1 - {lit}) | (c2 - {neg})
            # remove tautologies
            if not any(l[1:] if l.startswith("~") else "~"+l in new for l in new):
                resolvents.append(frozenset(new))
    return resolvents

# Try to derive empty clause (contradiction of ~R)
query = frozenset(["~R"])
agenda = kb + [query]
seen = set(agenda)
derived_empty = False
for _ in range(20):
    new_clauses = []
    for i, c1 in enumerate(agenda):
        for c2 in agenda[i+1:]:
            for r in resolve(c1, c2):
                if not r:          # empty clause
                    derived_empty = True
                    break
                if r not in seen:
                    seen.add(r)
                    new_clauses.append(r)
        if derived_empty:
            break
    if derived_empty or not new_clauses:
        break
    agenda.extend(new_clauses)

print("Derived empty clause (proved R)?", derived_empty)
```

2. Bayesian Inference (Naive Bayes style)

Classic Play-Tennis style example using Laplace-smoothed counts.

```
from collections import defaultdict
import math

# Tiny training set: (outlook, temperature, humidity, wind, play)
data = [
    ("Sunny","Hot","High","Weak","No"),
    ("Sunny","Hot","High","Strong","No"),
    ("Overcast","Hot","High","Weak","Yes"),
    ("Rain","Mild","High","Weak","Yes"),
    ("Rain","Cool","Normal","Weak","Yes"),
```

```
    ("Rain","Cool","Normal","Strong","No"),
    ("Overcast","Cool","Normal","Strong","Yes"),
    ("Sunny","Mild","High","Weak","No"),
    ("Sunny","Cool","Normal","Weak","Yes"),
    ("Rain","Mild","Normal","Weak","Yes"),
    ("Sunny","Mild","Normal","Strong","Yes"),
    ("Overcast","Mild","High","Strong","Yes"),
    ("Overcast","Hot","Normal","Weak","Yes"),
    ("Rain","Mild","High","Strong","No"),
]

def train_naive_bayes(data):
    class_counts = defaultdict(int)
    feat_counts = defaultdict(lambda: defaultdict(lambda: defaultdict(int)))
    for *feats, label in data:
        class_counts[label] += 1
        for i, v in enumerate(feats):
            feat_counts[i][v][label] += 1
    return class_counts, feat_counts

def predict(class_counts, feat_counts, x, alpha=1.0):
    """Return log-probabilities for each class (Laplace smoothed)."""
    total = sum(class_counts.values())
    scores = {}
    for c, cnt in class_counts.items():
        logp = math.log((cnt + alpha) / (total + alpha * len(class_counts)))
        for i, v in enumerate(x):
            # number of possible values for feature i (hard-coded for demo)
            n_vals = 3 if i < 3 else 2
            logp += math.log((feat_counts[i][v][c] + alpha) /
                             (cnt + alpha * n_vals))
        scores[c] = logp
    return scores

cc, fc = train_naive_bayes(data)
query = ("Sunny", "Cool", "High", "Strong")
print("Log-probabilities:", predict(cc, fc, query))
print("Predicted class:", max(predict(cc, fc, query), key=predict(cc, fc, query).get))
```

3. Tiny Neural Network (1-hidden-layer, NumPy)

A minimal feed-forward network trained with gradient descent on XOR.

```
import numpy as np

def sigmoid(z):
    return 1 / (1 + np.exp(-np.clip(z, -500, 500)))

def sigmoid_deriv(a):
    return a * (1 - a)

# XOR data
X = np.array([[0,0],[0,1],[1,0],[1,1]], dtype=float)
y = np.array([[0],[1],[1],[0]], dtype=float)

np.random.seed(42)
W1 = np.random.randn(2, 4) * 0.5   # 2 -> 4 hidden
b1 = np.zeros((1, 4))
W2 = np.random.randn(4, 1) * 0.5   # 4 -> 1
b2 = np.zeros((1, 1))

lr = 0.5
for epoch in range(5000):
    # forward
    z1 = X @ W1 + b1
    a1 = sigmoid(z1)
    z2 = a1 @ W2 + b2
    a2 = sigmoid(z2)
    # loss (MSE)
    loss = np.mean((a2 - y)**2)
    # backward
    dz2 = (a2 - y) * sigmoid_deriv(a2)
    dW2 = a1.T @ dz2
    db2 = np.sum(dz2, axis=0, keepdims=True)
    dz1 = (dz2 @ W2.T) * sigmoid_deriv(a1)
```

```
        dW1 = X.T @ dz1
        db1 = np.sum(dz1, axis=0, keepdims=True)
        # update
        W2 -= lr * dW2
        b2 -= lr * db2
        W1 -= lr * dW1
        b1 -= lr * db1

print("Final predictions:\n", np.round(a2, 3))
print("Targets:\n", y)
```

4. Simple Forward-Chaining Reasoner

A tiny rule engine that applies modus ponens style rules until quiescence.

```
# Rules: (antecedents_list, consequent)
rules = [
    (["human(Socrates)"], "mortal(Socrates)"),
    (["mortal(X)", "greek(X)"], "philosopher(X)"),   # simplified
    (["human(Socrates)"], "greek(Socrates)"),
]

facts = set(["human(Socrates)"])

def match(ante, facts):
    return all(a in facts for a in ante)

changed = True
while changed:
    changed = False
    for ante, cons in rules:
        if match(ante, facts) and cons not in facts:
            facts.add(cons)
            changed = True
            print("Derived:", cons)

print("Final facts:", facts)
```

These examples are deliberately minimal so they run in a few lines. They can be extended into full notebook-style explorations of the topics covered in the notes.

Index

A short topical index. Page numbers refer to this cleaned edition.

www.ingramcontent.com/pod-product-compliance
Lightning Source LLC
LaVergne TN
LVHW082347200926
848481LV00012B/3482
* 9 7 9 8 2 2 3 8 9 3 2 9 5 *